Emotionally
Literate

Behaviour
Management

A Training and Personal Development programme for teachers and those who support young people in schools.

Devised by Tina Rae

Visit us online at

ISBN 978-0-755202-84-3

Authors OnLine Ltd
19 The Cinques
Gamlingay, Sandy
Bedfordshire SG19 3NU
England

This book is also available in e-book format, details of which are available at
www.authorsonline.co.uk

Contents

Acknowledgements   2

A Personal Note   3

Introduction   4-5

References   6

Module 1   Identifying & labelling your Feelings   7-24

Module 2   Becoming a good listener   25-37

Module 3   Defining & Assessing yourself   38-49

Module 4   Managing Stress & Anger   50-61

Module 5   Managing Conflict   62-73

Module 6   Putting it all together – coaching   74-85

Module 7   10 Most useful strategies or Top Tips   86-102

Module 8   Action Planning   103-106

Acknowledgements

We would like to acknowledge the contributions made by the following people:

Patricia Black – Head teacher Chantry School
             – A college for SEN, London Borough of Hillingdon

Dave Bocock – Head teacher Bishopshalt High School, London Borough of Hillingdon

Jan Sargeant – Manager – Hillingdon Behaviour Support Team

Elizabeth Smith – Deputy Manager – Hillingdon Behaviour Support Team

Luke Jones – Advanced Skills Teacher (Drama) Bishopshalt High School

Terence Tiernan – Video Production

Students of Chantry & Bishopshalt School

A Personal Note

This course has been developed from a range of activities and courses that I have participated in and developed during the last 5 years as the Educational Psychologist for Chantry School.

The facilitators notes are consequently written as a 'script' i.e. what I would say if I were delivering each of the modules. If you are delivering the course, please feel free to change or adapt my words and styles to fit your own requirements.

I hope that this is a useful tool and that you enjoy delivering and working with this resource.

Tina Rae
April 2007

EMOTIONALLY LITERATE BEHAVIOUR MANAGEMENT

INTRODUCTION

This training course offers teachers a number of techniques and approaches aimed at improving the standards of pupils' behaviour in the school context. It does not promote or advocate one particular method or theory. However, it does place great importance on the notion of emotionally literate teachers who, themselves, have the skills which they can, in turn, model to the students that they teach. Behaviour management is a complex and difficult area for many teachers and the central aim of this course is to provide a series of practical and pragmatic training tools which are not, in any sense, prescriptive. What is important is that teachers, themselves, are given the opportunity to examine their own beliefs, pre-conceptions, attitudes and preferences. In this way, it is hoped that they can uncover and identify changes that they can make in order to further develop their skills in this area.

The course is designed to meet four central training objectives.

1. For teachers to develop an awareness of their own levels of emotional literacy and how this can impact both negatively and positively upon their own classroom management styles.
2. For teachers to identify the root causes of challenging behaviour and to discriminate accurately between what they can directly influence and what they can only influence indirectly.
3. For teachers to observe high quality classroom practice in which effective strategies and tools are used to manage the behaviour of the students.
4. For teachers to gain skills in assessing difficult situations and to further develop their own repertoire of coping strategies and support options.

The course is divided into eight modules as follows:

Module 1 – Identifying and Labelling your Feelings.
Module 2 – Becoming a Good Listener.
Module 3 – Defining and Asserting Yourself.
Module 4 – Managing Stress and Anger.
Module 5 – Managing Conflict.
Module 6 – Putting it all together – Coaching.
Module 7 – 10 Most Useful Strategies or Top Tips.
Module 8 – Action Planning.

At the outset it is vital to acknowledge the fact that teaching can be a stressful, tiring and, at times, a very difficult job. There are continued pressures to improve performance and the age old challenge of managing behaviour remains particularly relevant to teachers today given that the plethora of Government and Local Authority initiatives that can seem to, overwhelm the busy practitioner.

Behaviour clearly involves emotions. Teachers can be left feeling aggressive, demoralised and with a real sense of low morale, particularly when faced, on a daily basis, with a group of extremely challenging students. It is important at the outset to acknowledge that this is what we are going to focus on in this particular course. What is also important is to dispel the myth that there was a golden age when behaviour was good. We need to focus on what we have to work with now and the fact that the Government's agenda for inclusion has meant that even the most difficult and disaffected children now need to be included within the mainstream classroom context. We need to cut through the sense of isolation by building teams and a collegiate and emotionally literate approach towards ensuring that such students can be included.

What is also important is that teachers are given the opportunity to look at, first of all how they can change themselves. As Nelson Mandela said 'if we are expecting change in others we have to look at how we can first change ourselves'. This is difficult; behaviour is an emotional and emotive issue. What is vital is that the organisation within the school and the support structures, the value systems and the relationships are positive. There needs to be a sense of mutual respect between staff, parents and staff and students and staff. It is also vital to state the obvious; there are no easy solutions. What is vital is that teachers are given the time and opportunities to develop a sense of confidence and to also feel that they can be in control, both emotionally and intellectually within the classroom context.

Research has shown us very clearly that children imitate role models. They bring into school learnt behaviour from the home context. If their behaviour is unacceptable within this context, then it is vital that they are given the opportunity to develop more pro-social behaviours within the secure framework of school. Teachers who are calm, rational, friendly and enthusiastic provide appropriate models for students. We know that the main causes of inappropriate behaviour in the classrooms are four fold: Low self-esteem, lack of guidance within the home context, disaffection and a school ethos that concentrates on negative behaviour. It is vital that we reflect upon our own classroom management styles and that we also disassociate the behaviour from the child. We should never reject or discourage and we should also, at all times, remain positive. This is a tall order. It is not easy and it is important that this highlighted at the outset. However, the possibilities are endless for teachers to develop their own skills, self-confidence and their ability to cope more effectively within the most challenging classrooms.

It is hoped that this course, which focuses upon supporting the emotional development and support systems for teachers and schools will also encourage senior management teams within those contexts to review their policy and practice and the ways in which they support staff in effectively managing behaviour of students.

References

Ajmal, Y, & Rees, I. (Eds.) (2001) *Solution in Schools: Creative applications of solution focused brief thinking with young people and adults.* London BT Press.

Bolton, R. (1979) *People Skills: How to assert yourself, listen to others and resolve conflicts.* Englewood Cliffs, N.J. Prentice-Hall.

Burley-Allen, M. (1982) *Listening: the Forgotten Skill.* New York Wiley.

Cade, B & O'Hanlon, B. (1993) *A Brief Guide to Brief Therapy.* New York Norton.

Davies, M. (2004) *Test Your EQ- Find out how Emotionally Intelligent you really are.* London Piatkus.

Deutsch, M. (1973) *The Resolution of Conflict*, New Haven Yale University Press.

Egan, G. (1977) *You and Me: the skills of Communicating and Relating to others.* Monterey California Brooks /Cole.

Furman, B & Ahola, T. (1992) *Solution Talk: Hosting therapeutic conversations.* New York Norton.

Goleman, D. (1995) *Emotional Intelligence – why it can matter more than IQ.* London Bloomsbury

Goleman, D. (1999) *Working with Emotional Intelligence.* London Bloomsbury.

Lieberman, M & Hardie, M. (1981) *Resolving Family and other Conflicts.* Santa Cruz California. Unity Press.

Meichenbaum, D. (1983) *Coping with Stress.* London Century Publishing.

Nelson-Jones, R. (1986) *Human Relationship Skills Training and Self-help.* London Cassell Educational.

Novaco, R.W. (1977) *Stress Inoculation: a cognitive therapy for anger and its application in a case of depression* Journal of Consulting and Clinical Psychology 45. 600-608.

O'Connell, B., & Palmer, S. (Eds.) (2003) *Handbook of Solution Focused Therapy.* London Sage.

Rae, T. (2002) *Strictly Stress- A Stress Management Programme for High School Students.* Bristol Lucky Duck Publishing.

Rae, T. (2004) *Emotional Survival- An Emotional Literacy Course for High School Students.* Bristol Lucky Duck Publishing.

Rhodes, J., & Ajmal, Y. (1995) *Solution Focused Thinking in Schools.* London BT Press.

Seyle, H. (1974) *Stress Without Distress.* Sevenoaks: Hodder and Stroughton.
Stone, D, Patton, B., Heen, S., & Fisher, R. (2000) *Difficult Conversations: How to Discuss what matters Most.* London Penguin.

Emotionally Literate Behaviour Management

MODULE 1

Identifying and Labelling your Feelings

EMOTIONALLY LITERATE BEHAVIOUR MANAGEMENT

MODULE 1 – IDENTIFYING AND LABELLING YOUR FEELINGS

Introduction

During recent years there has been a wealth of research in the area of emotional literacy. This has led to what can only be described as a plethora of resources and materials for teachers to use in order to attempt to develop these kinds of skills in the pupils they teach. The government's agenda of social inclusion and the development from the DfES of a social, emotional and behavioural skills curriculum for students throughout all key stages, has resulted in a recognition of the fact that these are vital skills for children and young people to acquire if they are going to eventually be academically successful and be able to function within a range of social contexts. However, in my view what seems to be missing here is the need to focus, prior to delivering such curriculums, on the actual skills that teachers themselves have. It seems logical to me that if teachers are emotionally literate or 'intelligent', then they will generally have greater impact upon the pupils that they teach and they will certainly be able to foster the kinds of skills that we are looking for more successfully.

I would like to highlight from the outset, the fact that what will also make a difference to teachers themselves is the emotional climate of the school in which they teach and whether or not the school presents as an emotionally literate, safe and nurturing environment. I would suggest that in order for us all to develop these skills, we need to be working within non-judgemental and democratic contexts. Consequently, the main focus here will be on presenting you with opportunities to further understand this concept of emotional literacy and to reflect upon, think about and perhaps further develop your own skills. The aims here are really quite simple: overall I'd like you to be able to really understand what it is to be an emotionally literate person and to gain a further insight into your own development in this area and the ways in which you may wish to further develop your competences in order be both successful or more successful in the classroom and also in your own social contexts.

So why do I think that this is important for teachers? Well, we know that children's emotional literacy is related to their mental health so it would seem logical to assume that the same relationship would exist for their teachers, parents and carers as well. If we go back as far as 1989 and the Elton Report, we can see that the role of positive relationships in the teaching and learning environment was highlighted even then and specifically the ways in which teachers could be and needed to be, fully effective. I quote,
'To be fully effective, teachers need the ability to relate to young people, to encourage them in good behaviour and learning and to deal calmly but firmly with in appropriate or disruptive behaviour, establishing good relationships with pupils, encouraging them to learn and to behave well, have always been essential parts of the teacher's work. This cannot be achieved by talking at children, but by working with them.' (Elton Report 1969 – Page 67-68)

Now I know that this seems to be stating the obvious but developing and maintaining positive and caring relationships with pupils is important and the emotional connection in social education, I feel, is just as important as pupil's cognitive education. However, the kind of conflict between caring and the pressures of the market place are a cause of emotional dissonance and stress amongst teachers. There are enormous difficulties in dealing with and in coping with so-called 'difficult children' in stressful situations on a daily basis. Teachers are somehow expected, as if by magic, to be able to emotionally sustain themselves and remain secure, confident and emotionally intact even when faced with many pressures and stresses, not only from the pupils and the way in which they behave themselves but also from the plethora of initiatives which seem to be pouring out from the DfES.

I want to acknowledge the fact that being a teacher and managing others' emotions and behaviour on a daily basis in this really intensive manner involves a great deal of emotional labour. This is perhaps the main reason why I feel that it is absolutely essential for teachers to have the opportunity and time to both self reflect and nurture their own skills, their own emotional competences and ability to cope effectively on a daily basis. So, in this initial session I am hoping there will be an opportunity for you to begin to consider your own levels of emotional literacy and to begin to understand the need and importance of being able to identify and label your own feelings. If we don't develop these skills then I fear that this will have, or may already be having, a negative impact upon our ability to develop relationships, not just with the pupils but with each other. I would also suggest, further to this, that our relationships with each other and with ourselves are what we should focus on initially if we are really going to be effective as teachers in the classroom on a longer and more sustained basis. We cannot manage the behaviour and emotional states of our students unless we can firstly effectively manage our own behaviours and responses.

So, in this session, the main aim is to consider the nature of emotional literacy, what it is, what it means for us and to us and to also then reflect upon our own skills in this area. But, before we actually turn to ourselves, it may be useful to break the ice a little.

Activity 1

Icebreaker

In this first icebreaker activity, I would like everyone just to turn to the person sitting next to them and to question each other in order to find out three things that you both have in common. Discuss in detail and to try and find out three things that you both have in common/that you are both interested in. It may be that you've both been to the same place on holiday; it may be that you both like drinking malt whisky; whatever it is I would then like you to feed that information back to the whole group.

Activity 2

Now that we have introduced ourselves to one another and hopefully feel a little more relaxed, I would like to continue with the second activity which I hope will further clarify this notion of emotional literacy. I call this a 'story time for grownups' and it is a story. I know teachers are very often required to read stories to students and they obviously expect them to listen and pay attention and possibly even answer questions afterwards and discuss some of the issues raised. That is exactly what we are going to do in this session so I would like you to listen very, very carefully. Here's the story and I really would reinforce with you the importance of listening as there will be some activities for you to undertake afterwards!

"Once upon a time (or should I say quite a while ago) there was a big storm on the island of Ingaros in the South Pacific which was a great shame really, given the fact that Maureen and Angus Reed had just arrived for their annual two-week break. On that particular morning, they had been out for a pre-lunch walk along the northern coastal path which was quite a good idea when reflecting upon the sort of diet they had been coping with at the all-inclusive hotel. Those sorts of breakfasts were certainly not the 'norm' at home and would require at least three hours of forced marching in order to burn off the immense calorie intake.

As they walked along the northern ridge, the sun was beating down upon their heads and both Maureen and Angus felt the need to stop for a drink of water. 'I can feel myself dehydrating', said Angus. 'It must be the effects of last night's alcohol intake'. He gulped down the water and then handed the bottle to Maureen. 'Thanks', she said somewhat sarcastically, 'You haven't exactly left me with enough to quench my thirst'. 'Don't start', said Angus. He was just about to launch into his usual tirade about how selfish she was and how she always had to consider her own needs first, when he suddenly noticed something out to sea. He stood still and stared straight ahead, his mouth slightly gaping. 'What is it?' said Maureen, sounding confused and somewhat perturbed that he had stopped mid flow as she was secretly looking forward to the ensuing argument. She turned round following his gaze out to sea. 'Oh my God!' she said. The storm was clearly visible on the horizon: the dark clouds had formed within what seemed like seconds and the thunder had erupted into great blasts overhead. 'I think we'd better run for it', said Angus. 'We seem to be far too exposed on this ridge'. Maureen nodded in agreement. 'Look down there in the valley – there is a bridge across to some caves. We would probably be better off if we got down there. At least we could get some shelter'. Come on then', said Angus, 'Let's make a run for it'.

They proceeded to scramble down the rough goat track until they reached the bridge which was a rather rickety affair. Maureen thought that it wasn't likely to hold their weight but also thought she had better keep her thoughts to herself. She'd only be accused of being negative yet again. Angus ran ahead of her and shouted back, 'Come on, hurry up, the storm seems to be getting stronger – head for the cave'. He ran on to the bridge and straight across it. Just as he reached the other end, the bridge collapsed entirely, leaving Maureen stranded on the opposite side of the ravine. Angus turned round and watched in utter horror as it shattered into pieces. The wood was absolutely rotten. Maureen stood still, biting her lip. For one moment she considered trying to jump across and then immediately thought the better of it. You'd need to be an Olympic medallist to cope with that. Angus shouted to her, 'Get back behind the trees – find the biggest ones and sit between them with your back against the trunk. Go on – hurry up'. He ran off into the cave.

Fortunately, he had been carrying the rucksack containing all the food for their lunch and he now thought that he would set down, dry off and have a little picnic. He remembered that he had packed four cans of best bitter and felt quite pleased with himself.

Maureen ran back and found a clump of rather over-large trees and sat down. She did not feel at all happy nor particularly safe from the storm. 'He's the one that's entirely selfish', she thought, 'and I've broken three nails scrambling down that hill'. Just then she heard a rustle in the undergrowth behind her. She sat up feeling startled and frightened thinking that there would be a snake nearby, and then let out a big sigh of relief as she saw the head waiter from the hotel approaching her. He was absolutely gorgeous – tall, handsome and with quite exceptional pectoral muscles. 'Hello, Romeo, she said. What on earth are you doing out in a storm like this?' 'Well, he replied, 'I saw you both leaving for your walk and I ran after you because I had heard the appalling weather forecast. I was hoping to catch up with you both and warn you. 'Are you okay?' 'Yes, I am now', she said. 'But where is your husband?' 'Oh, she replied looking somewhat dejected. 'He fell down the ravine as he was trying to cross the bridge. He died instantly and his body was washed away in the storm waters'. 'Oh, dear', said Romeo. 'Well I suppose it's not such a bad thing really'. 'What do you mean?' said Maureen sounding rather shocked. 'Well, I've always fancied you – now that he's out of the picture we should be able to get to know each other properly. What do you think?' 'Okay', she said and jumped directly into his arms, kissing his neck and chest repeatedly.

I'm afraid the rest of it simply can't be recorded here. End of story."

Now clearly this story is tongue in cheek but there is a purpose to it so I would ask you to bear with me. I'd like you to work together in this next activity but also to initially work on your own in terms of thinking about the characters within this story. I'd like you to identify who you think is the nastiest person in this story; the second nastiest; and the third nastiest and in your own minds I would like you to justify this ranking process. What are your reasons for placing the characters in this order of nastiness? Now, I'm going to ask you to arrange yourselves into groups of, six to eight and within those groups I'd like you to place yourselves in a circle sitting as for a Circle Time session. Then nominate one person to begin who feels that they've already minds completed their personal ranking process. I'd then like this person to begin by explaining their views to the person next to them – either right or left – it doesn't matter which way you go round the circle. The person who is listening will then need to summarise the views of the first speaker prior to giving their own to the person sitting directly next to them in the circle. So, in effect, what should be happening here is that everyone in the group should have the opportunity to give their views and everyone should be summarising at least one member's views prior to giving their own. At the end of this I'm going to ask each of the groups if you can come to some agreement in terms of ordering your characters into first, second and third nastiest.

Activity 3

Although I recognise that this is fun activity and there is hopefully quite a lot of humour involved in this story, there is a serious purpose here. That is to highlight the kind of skills that you were using in the activity. When you think about it and reflect upon it, what I was asking you to do was to withhold gratification to allow other people to speak, to listen appropriately, to maintain appropriate eye contact, not to butt in, not to shout someone down, to be able to cope with feelings of anxiety when someone whom you know very well or whose views you respect happens to differ to you in their opinions about something. I was asking you to be active listeners, to sensitively consider each other's feelings and view points, to make use of simple social skills such as taking turns, and appropriate body language when someone else is talking. Some of those skills are quite basic and some are more sophisticated. I think what is interesting here is that these are the kinds of skills that we expect children to have developed and that they need in order to access the curriculum presented to them in today's school contexts.

I suppose we presume that they've learnt these skills at home or we presume that they would have picked them up anyway somehow as if by magic. And it's not easy; it's very, very difficult! Even within the adult context we find ourselves shouting over each other or talking over each other. And yet, these are skills that we expect children to have and to demonstrate on a daily basis in the classroom. We'll all stand up, we'll talk, we'll read a story, we'll be asking them to participate in certain activities that demand many of these skills and we'll be come distressed and upset if they don't display them in a way that we deem to be appropriate. Yet, I think I'd argue that really we need to be looking at our own skills first and we also need to be reflecting upon the fact that this is not always easy. It's not always easy to wait your turn; it's not always easy to withhold gratification; it's not always easy to manage difficult and uncomfortable feelings, particularly in a public context.

It may be helpful if we now thought-storm the following question: What kinds of skills do we think that we were using there? I will act as the scribe for your ideas.

If we look at the resulting list I would suggest that the kinds of skills that we were using in this activity are those of emotional literacy. We can focus on a useful definition by Gillian Shotten (2003 – Page 1) where she suggested that emotional literacy could be defined 'as the ability to recognise, understand, handle and appropriately express your emotions' and this includes the following:

- being aware of what you are feeling
- understanding why you might be feeling that way
- knowing the most effective way for expressing your feelings and being able actually carry out this response
- understanding and taking into account the feelings of others and adjusting your responses accordingly.

I think that these four areas of emotional literacy are the key ones on which we need to focus.

Activity 4

Listening to your Feelings

We know that feelings are really important and particularly in the area of relationships. If we are going to be able to develop, maintain and, if necessary, end relationships then we need very much to be clued into our own feelings and emotions, to really understand them and respond to them in an effective manner. Richard Nelson Jones in his book, 'Human Relationship Skills' identified the reasons why it is particularly important for us to be responsive to the flow of our feelings. He recorded seven main reasons.

The first one is that we need to be responsive to this flow of feelings because it can help us to acknowledge any kind of sense of liking or attraction that we have for someone. Then there is this issue of spontaneity. If we are in touch with our feelings we are free to be more creative and respond in a fresher way in our relationships. Then there is sensuality which, on one level, means touch but affectionate use of physical contact can be affirming and may not need to have a sexual goal although it may obviously involve sexuality. Then there is rationality. What he argues is that, if you are truly in touch with what you feel about situations, you are less likely to be reacting to the prohibitions and inhibitions you've probably unthinkingly learnt from others. It can cut across much of the self-defeating thinking that makes for rational feelings and behaviour.

Also there is existential awareness, i.e. really being fully in touch with your feelings entails acknowledging the reality of your finitude and this may lead us to feel more urgent about making the most of our relationships. Then there is the issue of finding meaning. We are meaning-seeking beings and happiness and fulfilment entails finding meaning in life. If we don't have this sense of meaning, then we would only experience feelings of emptiness, apathy and despair. Finally, there is this notion of identity and according to Richard Nelson Jones; relationships are most satisfactory when both of you have a secure sense of your own identities as separate individuals. We're going to do an exercise now which is designed to help us become aware of how we are grounded in what could be called our 'bodily feelings'.

First of all I would like everyone to sit in a quiet place, close your eyes for about five minutes and then try to tune into the sensations you are experiencing within your own bodies. I'd like you to try and focus on what your body is actually feeling rather than on what you are thinking. You may be thinking this is stupid, this is daft, but please try and put those thoughts aside and actually really think what is my body feeling; what am I actually feeling at this present moment in time? Secondly, I'd like you to focus on the physical sensations in each of these parts of your body just for about one minute each. First of all start off with your arms; your head; the trunk of your body; your legs. Next I would like you to keep your eyes closed and for the next three to five minutes just focus purely on the sensations of your breathing. I would like you to give me some feedback on those three activities. How difficult or easy was it to focus on what your body was feeling rather than on what you were thinking and what kinds of physical sensations did you experience when focusing on those different areas of your body? How did it feel to be focusing purely on the sensations of your breathing? Finally, I would like you to just quickly write down the bodily sensations attached to you experiencing the following emotions:

- anger
- despair
- happiness
- fear

Hopefully, what we should be able to see from these kinds of exercises is that listening to feelings requires us not just to be aware of bodily sensations but also the capacity to identify and label our feelings accurately. For example, if Richard asks Emily out for a date and she very nicely and politely, but firmly, declines his offer there are a range of possible feelings that he might experience as a result of this. He could be hurt, he could be very angry or humiliated. He could feel very tense or he could be quite relieved or even optimistic. He has got some choice about the feelings he experiences and it depends, to a large extent, on the way in which he interprets Emily's refusal. He could choose to think that it's absolutely awful – nothing as bad or humiliating as this has ever happened to me before in my life – or he could think well, she's just thick and stupid and has made the wrong decision. Or, alternatively, that she's entitled to take this position and I can't always be successful so I'll pop off and try somewhere else.

Clearly, these choices in the interpretation will contribute to the feelings that he would experience, either of being anxious or depressed or feeling angry in the second interpretation or feeling more confident and optimistic in the last one. Following on from this what I'm going to ask you to consider the importance of, is the need to try and identify and label what you actually feel and in order to do this it is important to have a vocabulary with which to describe feelings. This is one of the key skills of emotional literacy that I think we all need to have. As well as teaching our students this vocabulary, we will need to make sure that we have developed it ourselves. I know that for those who are trained to become counsellors or psychotherapists, some of their training actually involves building a repertoire of feeling words so that they can help their clients to feel really accurately understood. It is vital that we actually learn to identify and label feelings and that we have as many of these feelings words or words for describing our feelings as we can in our repertoire. I have consequently provided you with a list of feelings words which we may use in subsequent activities and these are as follows:

Accepted	Adventurous	Affectionate
Aggressive	Ambitious	Angry
Anxious	Apathetic	Appreciated
Assertive	Attractive	Bored
Carefree	Cautious	Cheerful
Competitive	Confident	Confused
Contented	Co-operative	Daring
Decisive	Dependent	Depressed
Discontented	Embarrassed	Energetic
Envious	Excitable	Fit
Free	Friendly	Frightened
Grieving	Guilt-free	Guilty
Happy	Humiliated	Hurt
Indecisive	Independent	Inferior
Insecure	Interested	Involved
Irresponsible	Jealous	Joyful
Lonely	Loved	Loving
Optimistic	Outgoing	Pessimistic
Powerful	Powerless	Rejected
Relaxed	Resentful	Responsible
Sad	Secure	Shy
Stressed	Strong	Superior
Supportive	Suspicious	Tense
Tired	Trusting	Unambitious
Unappreciated	Unassertive	Unattractive
Under-confident	Uneasy	Unfit
Unfree	Unfriendly	Unloved
Unsupported	Unwanted	Uptight
Vulnerable	Wanted	Weak
Worried		

Please feel free to make any additions!

Activity 5

Identifying and Labelling your Feelings

I'd like you to have a go at this exercise on your own initially and then to perhaps share your responses with a partner or colleague. There are a range of twelve sentences that I would like you to complete regarding your feelings within the context of relationships. Focus on how you really feel rather than on your own thoughts about the other person. So complete each of the sentences by writing down two alternative words or phrases that would perhaps describe most accurately the way that you feel.

1. When someone ignores me I feel ………………………………………………..

2. When someone cries I feel ………………………………………………………

3. When someone praises me I feel ....

4. When someone talks about themselves all the time I feel ....

5. When someone gets mad at me I feel..

6. When someone attracts me I feel ....

7. When someone really cares for me I feel ....

8. When someone acts superior to me I feel ....

9. When someone breaks a confidence I feel ....

10. When someone if very late for an appointment or meeting I feel............

11. When I go into a group of strangers I feel ....

12. When someone really listens to me and understands me I feel ....

I'd like you to then think about these situations identifying any in which you have conflicting feelings and discuss this with your colleague. We will then have some feedback to the group as a whole.

Activity 6

Describing Yourself

In this activity what I would like you to do is look at the list of feeling words that have been provided and to pick out ten that you think best describe you at this current time. Obviously you can include words that aren't on the list. What I would like you to do then is to write 'positive' after those feelings that you like within yourself and 'negative' about those that you dislike. So you will have two columns in which you put feelings i.e. positive or negative. It might then be helpful to discuss responses with a partner and then to think about whether or not you have any similarities or differences in terms of your predominant feelings. It also might be helpful now to begin to think more: what is it about the context in which we find ourselves? It may be impacting upon our feelings or creating these feelings or reinforcing them in either a positive or a negative way. Finally, we can all discuss responses in a general feedback session and to really think about our own levels of confidence in this area and to perhaps consider overall how you feel about your skills: what you think you might need to develop in the future in order to be more successful at listening to feelings and recognising what they are, where they come from and how you can perhaps manage them more effectively.

Final Take-home Tasks

These take home tasks require you to now have a go at doing a couple of self-reflection activities away from the group in order to think a little more deeply and a little more personally about your own skills and things that you may wish to change in the future. The first activity encourages us to consider how we can alter our patterns of behaviour and it's basically a five-step process as follows:

Step A involves you in writing down emotions that you have likely to experience in your workplace, e.g. anger, joy, anxiety, contentment, enthusiasm, fear, sickness, frustration, etc.

Step B asks you to identify behaviours or patterns of behaviours which accompany the emotions that you are most likely to encounter at work.

Step C asks you to then list your corresponding actions for these emotions that you have recorded on your list.

Step D then asks you to consider any unhelpful patterns of behaviour – what is happening and why. Why is this unhelpful? What is it stopping you doing? What is it stopping you changing?

Step E then asks you to visualise and, if effect, choose a new response.

This idea of visualisation, of visualising yourself in the old situation hopefully allows for a re-evaluation of any negative self-beliefs and it is through such a process I think that we can move forward and make changes. It is an opportunity to choose a new response to the same situation and then have a go at trying it out. It's a challenge! It's something that's quite tricky. When we are asked to change specific behaviours and need to think about and do something new, this can be difficult for many of us. If we are set a cognitive task, e.g. learning a new computer programme, then we tend to simply get on with it or read the manual, learn how to do it and have a go. But in this case, what I'm asking you to do is undertake some emotional learning. I might be asking you to think about how you manage your anger or how your anger management patterns or behaviours need to be adjusted and instantly this is more of a challenge because it feels somehow more personal.

The second activity I'd like you to have a go at is the questionnaire, 'How Emotionally Literate Are You?' This isn't intended as any kind of scientific tool but it is intended to prompt your thinking and to help you in this process of self-reflection. What are your skills? How good are you in all of these areas – being self-aware, regulating yourself, motivating yourself, empathising with others, your social skills? What do you need to improve on and how can you make the kinds of changes you may need to make or wish to make in the future? It would be really helpful if you could have a go at doing both of these because this is the kind of process we need to engage in if we are going to develop our skills still further and if we truly are going to become the kind of emotionally literate teachers who can manage, identify, label and manage our feelings in the most effective way.

Module 1 – Activity 4

Feelings List		
Accepted	Adventurous	Affectionate
Aggressive	Ambitious	Angry
Anxious	Apathetic	Appreciated
Assertive	Attractive	Bored
Carefree	Cautious	Cheerful
Competitive	Confident	Confused
Contented	Co-operative	Daring
Decisive	Dependent	Depressed
Discontented	Embarrassed	Energetic
Envious	Excitable	Fit
Free	Friendly	Frightened
Grieving	Guilt-free	Guilty
Happy	Humiliated	Hurt
Indecisive	Independent	Inferior
Insecure	Interested	Involved
Irresponsible	Jealous	Joyful
Lonely	Loved	Loving
Optimistic	Outgoing	Pessimistic
Powerful	Powerless	Rejected
Relaxed	Resentful	Responsible
Sad	Secure	Shy
Stressed	Strong	Superior
Supportive	Suspicious	Tense
Tired	Trusting	Unambitious
Unappreciated	Unassertive	Unattractive
Under-confident	Uneasy	Unfit
Unfree	Unfriendly	Unloved
Unsupported	Unwanted	Uptight
Vulnerable	Wanted	Weak
Worried		

Module 1 – Activity 5

Identifying and Labelling your Feelings

Complete each of the sentences by writing down two alternative words or phrases that would perhaps describe most accurately the way that you feel.

1. When someone ignores me I feel ....

2. When someone cries I feel ....

3. When someone praises me I feel ....

4. When someone talks about themselves all the time I feel ....

5. When someone gets mad at me I feel ....

6. When someone attracts me I feel ....

7. When someone really cares for me I feel ....

8. When someone acts superior to me I feel ....

9. When someone breaks a confidence I feel ....

10. When someone if very late for an appointment or meeting I feel ....

11. When I go into a group of strangers I feel ....

12. When someone really listens to me and understands me I feel ....

Any Conflicting Feelings?

-

-

-

-

EMOTIONAL LITERACY EXERCISE

Step A

- Write down emotions that you are likely to experience in your workplace: anger, joy, anxiety, contentment, enthusiasm, fear, sickness, frustration etc.

Step B

- What behaviours/patterns of behaviour accompany the emotions that you're most likely to encounter at work?

Step C

- For the strongest emotions on the list, what are your corresponding actions?

Step D

- Explore your unhelpful patterns of behaviour – what is happening and why?

Step E

♦ Visualise and choose a new response. Visualising yourself in the old situation allows for a re-evaluation of any negative self-beliefs that were forms or beliefs about others. You can then choose a new response to the chain of emotions triggered by the situation should you encounter them again.

Module 1 – Emotionally Literacy Behaviour Management

How is your Emotional Literacy?
A self-reflection activity
Take home Task 2

How do you rate? Read each statement and tick against each scale:

0 – not at all   3 = sometimes   5 = always

Under each heading add your score to get a total score out of 20.

Key Skills
Awareness of feelings

	0	1	2	3	4	5
You know what you are feeling						
You can label your feelings						
You know when your feelings affect your work						
You know when your feelings affect your relationships						

Total score   /20

Personal insight

	0	1	2	3	4	5
You know your strengths						
You know your weaknesses						
You can take constructive criticism or feedback from others						
You know when you've done something well and can feel good about yourself						

Total score   /20

Self-assurance

	0	1	2	3	4	5
You act confidently in most situations						
You stick up for things you think are right						
Other people think you are confident						
You could easily name three things you are good at even when you are down						

Total Score   /20

How is your Emotional Literacy?
Continued

Self-regulation or control

	0	1	2	3	4	5
You can stop yourself when you know you're behaving in way that will cause problems (for you and others)						
You can keep calm under pressure						
You can handle uncomfortable feelings well						
You can use strategies to reduce stress and anxiety						

Total score   /20

Authenticity

	0	1	2	3	4	5
When you say you'll do something you do it						
You don't say or act one thing and then do another						
You can admit your mistakes						
You can stand up for what you think even if you are in the minority						

Total score   /20

Accountability

	0	1	2	3	4	5
You can take responsibility for your behaviour and actions						
You keep your promises						
You admit when you have made a mistake						
Your friends and family know they can count on you						

Total score   /20

How is your Emotional Literacy?
Continued

Flexibility

	0	1	2	3	4	5
You can cope with changes to your day						
You don't get stressed by change and can go with the flow						
You like to be creative and think of new ways of doing things						
You see the benefit in trying new things and are eager to do so						

Total score   /20

Self-motivation

	0	1	2	3	4	5
You like to achieve your best						
You like to get things done						
You are committed to your relationships						
You'll keep going even if things get tough						
You are optimistic and look for opportunities before you look for problems						

Total score   /20

Stop and Think

What are your highest scores?

Where are your lowest scores?

Which is your best key skill and which is your weakest?

Try to think of three things that you could do in order to improve your skills:

1. _____

2. _____

3. _____

Emotionally Literate Behaviour Management

MODULE 2

Becoming a Good Listener

EMOTIONALLY LITERATE BEHAVIOUR MANAGEMENT

MODULE 2: BECOMING A GOOD LISTENER

Introduction

An emotionally literate person is someone who is a good listener. Being a good listener is definitely related to being relaxed and also talking about yourself. The less energy you spend on worrying about what other's reactions might be to you or the way you think, or feel, or act, then the more time you've got to devote to actually listening to them and their concerns and their views. We tend to think that we're naturally good listeners and people have this idea that if you're a teacher then that's definitely a skill that you must have developed. There's a kind of illusion that we, as teachers or educational professionals, have good listening skills and that it's something that is quite natural to us. In this session what I am aiming to do is to just put a little pin prick into that bubble of confidence about our listening skills. I think that when we actually self-reflect a little more we may find that our skills aren't as highly developed as we may like to think. This is an area that we need to be confident about but confident that we can always make improvements and changes, and that we can always further develop our skills. If we are able to do that then our teaching in the classroom will be more effective. Also, our relationships with each other and the ways in which we interact with each other as a staff team will improve significantly.

I would suggest that listening is an extremely powerful way of affirming another human being. I think we know that when children are growing up the quality of listening that the adults give them is vital for their psychological development and their mental health. Those that have been well listened to are not only likely to feel accepted by others but they are also, I think, more likely to be able to accept themselves. They have also been given the opportunity to safely express and explore the way that they feel about things and people and this, in turn, helps them to acquire that capacity of inner listening, i.e. listening to themselves and being able to trust their own feelings and their own reactions. That is an essential part of what I would define as 'outer listening', i.e. the ability to listen to others. It is the children who have not been adequately listened to who are likely to be out of touch with their feelings and they are also more likely to be afraid and anxious and even aggressive and violent at times. I think that good listening not only can this affirm the core of another person's being but bad listening can totally disconfirm it. When this is something that is perpetuated on a regular basis in its most aggressive and violent form, this is a kind of psychological violence (even if it's often unintended). I would suggest that we have a real duty as teachers and professionals working with children in the educational field to ensure that t we do not perpetuate this kind of psychological violence. We need to be making sure that we are providing our students and each other with opportunities to be listened to in an appropriate way, in a 'good' way so that what we are doing is affirming one another on a continual basis. What I'm not suggesting here is that we need to be listening too much. The alternative, I suppose, to a good listener is someone who listens to someone to such an extent that they generally tend to be on the receiving end of ear-pushing on a very regular basis. Also, I would suggest that listening too much can be a form of defensiveness i.e. when what we do is that we allow others to take all of the risks involved in revealing themselves in the way they think and feel about things whilst we conceal ourselves. In a way this is another form of psychological violence on the other end of the continuum. I would consider that misuse of listening in this way, would impede rather than facilitate the development of genuine relationships.

What I would like to do in this session is to begin to prompt your thinking and awareness as to your own skills in this area and to also highlight some of the possible sources of interference that may be experienced and to ask you to self-reflect in a more detailed way about whether or not you are a safe listener. Also, I think that a useful outcome here would be to be able to understand the importance of really understanding other people's frame of reference, getting into their world. So what we are going to be doing in this module are quite a few exercises which will hopefully help us to consider the importance of disciplining our listening and developing the kinds of skills that help us to really understand another's world. This is the key concept here because if we can do this in our relationships as professionals but we will also do it with parents and with students. Overall, I think that this will make for a safer more nurturing and more mutually respectful context in which we can work. I think there are key skills here of staying in and checking out, summarising another's frame of reference and of disciplining our own body language so that we demonstrate attention and interest. I think that as teachers, we tend to think that we've got these skills, but I would ask you to consider the following questions: When did you receive training in becoming a good listener? When have you ever had access to time like this in which to think about it and totally self-reflect on your own skills and development in this area? Was it included in your initial teacher training? Has it been included in professional development training since then? I hope it has and I hope that this session today will usefully and constructively build upon anything that you've covered to date. Also, that it will really start to help you to develop a more extensive repertoire of effective listening skills.

Activity 1

As an initial awareness raising exercise I would like you to complete the questionnaire. You're going to be presented with a list of 22 statements and I would like you to write down next to each statement whether you consider it to be true or false. Use the initials 't' or 'f' against each of the statements and then discuss your responses to these and see if we can identify some common ground here.

The statements are as follows:

1. Children are taught when they're little to be good listeners.
2. People's thinking can interfere with the way they listen.
3. Listening is an entirely natural activity

4. If you are able to listen to others then you should be able to listen to yourself
5. People can sometimes resist listening to other people who blame and get angry with them
6. You never have to be self-disciplined to be a good listener
7. People are far more likely to talk to others with whom they feel secure and safe than with those whom they don't
8. It is always up to the individual person to communicate exactly what they want
9. People who have something that they can't wait to say generally listen well
10. Some people listen too much simply because they are afraid of disclosing anything about themselves
11. An important aspect in developing trust is to be able to listen and then keep someone else's confidences or secrets.

So, what do I think?

When we talk, we sometimes send mixed messages and these can be difficult for the listener to understand. People are more likely to hear the message that corresponds with their own view of themselves and not hear those which challenge their views. Repeatedly not listening to or understanding another person can be viewed as a form of psychological violence. Listening to other people involves paying attention to their voice quality and body language as well as to what they say. People who tend to feel emotional about issues are generally good listeners. Being an effective listener entails making a series of correct choices in receiving what is being said by the individual concerned. Being tired doesn't affect the quality of your listening. The amount that an individual feels about his or herself is likely to influence the amount that others tell them in return. Talking is more important than listening.

Activity 2

What Interferes With Your Listening

In an ideal world when we're talking we would be readily and easily understood by everyone listening to us, but in real life we know that it's not as simple as that. Basically what tends to happen is that certain things will interfere with that listening process. When things are going well and we can hear someone loud and clear, it's not a problem, but on many other occasions there is likely to be poor reception due to some kind of interference, almost like listening to a radio and receiving a radio message. The reasons for the interference can be located on either the sender's radio, the receiver's radio or both. There are certain talkers characteristics which I think may be sources of interference and these will obviously impede accurate listening. These include the following:

- Lack of clarity regarding the intentions of a specific message
- Material mistakenly being left out of a message
- Material that is left out because of incorrect assumption that it is known
- Material that is left out because of the incorrect assumption being made that this material is already known

A message can be encoded rather than communicated absolutely directly. There can be a lack of matching vocal and bodily actions with the verbal communication; these two just do not seem to co-exist happily. An individual can have vocal or bodily mannerisms which discourage the listening. The speaker may have a heavy accent or poor command of language or a speech impediment. There may be shyness or lack of confidence or anxiety and tension, or anger and aggression. The speaker may use blame language and the speaker may, at times, engage in a competitive power contest or focus on awkward topic areas which make the listener feel uncomfortable, for example, sexuality or race etc. Overall, what is important to remember is that many of the internal sources of interference that we experience are definitely related to our own levels of confidence. We know that our levels of self-acceptance and confidence are generally related to how well we were listened to when we were growing up. What is important is to be aware of the fact that these can be remedied, altered, or ultimately changed. We are all open to change or the possibility of change and personal development in this way. As a starting point we can all explore our sources of interference to listening accurately.

This is a paired exercise. I would like everyone to feedback once they have completed it. I would like you to try and focus upon the following.

1. Try and write down or discuss as many of the intentional barriers and filters that you have experienced when attempting to listen to others. So anything that has interfered with your listening is an intentional barrier or filter.
2. Can you discuss a time when your own or another person's emotions have interfered with your capacity to listen. Can you give examples?
3. Are there certain types or categories of people to whom you find it difficult to listen? Can you describe them and why this may be the case?
4. Are there any words, phrases or attitudes from others that tend to trigger off in your resistance to listening? Can you describe them?
5. Are there any particular areas or topics which you find it difficult to listen to?
6. Are there any other sources of interference that you have experienced with your listening?

Once these have been answered in pairs it would be useful to have a plenary in which we share our ideas.

Activity 3

Being a good or a bad listener

I think the last activity shows us that we can actually change sources of interference. We can avoid them, we can recognise them, we can analyse them, we can push them away, and we can actually know ourselves even better so that we can ensure this interference is conscious rather than unconscious. Ultimately, what we need to do is to be in control and to choose to listen well. We do have choice here and that is something that empowers us in all areas of our lives but particularly in the emotional field.

What I would like you to do now is to again work in pairs and consider the following:

1. Think of at least three individuals in your current or past life that you would regard as being really good at listening and three that you consider to be very poor at listening.
2. Then I would like you to write down on one half of the sheet of A4 paper all the characteristics you had associated with a good listener and then on the other side of the page all of those that you had associated with a bad listener.
3. I would then like you to have a short period of self-reflection assessing your own skills, resources and deficits as a listener looking at these two lists which ones would apply to you and which ones do you think you could change and what do you need to do in order to make such changes.

It would be really helpful to have feedback within your pair and then to feedback to the group as a whole so that we can begin to identify the characteristics of a good listener.

Activity 4

Are you a safe listener?

I think it is important to think about how safe we are as listeners, both in our interactions with students and in our interactions with parents and colleagues. Often, in our everyday interactions and conversations, we don't facilitate very well another person's feelings of safety and security and we don't very often successfully encourage them to talk. How much talk in a classroom is done by the teacher? How much listening is done by the teacher and how much talk and listening is done by the students? It would be quite interesting to analyse that and I think that there has been a great deal of research to show that, particularly at the secondary level, there is far more talking done by teachers as opposed to listening and communicating with students. I think we can also make a distinction between what would possibly be called a therapeutic conversation and a social conversation.

In a therapeutic conversation, the therapist will be listening extremely carefully to the client and carefully re-framing and reinforcing the conversation, making sure that they have really listened and are accurately reporting back.

Within a social conversation, the process could be described rather cynically as two people taking turns to simply exercise their egos. Overall, what is true, is that in whatever context we are talking if we are doing this successfully then we need to have the psychological space in which to do it. People are given the quantity of space in which to talk if the other person doesn't simply hog the conversation. Also a good quality of psychological space is given when the listener chooses to show respect and value the importance of the other person's thoughts and feelings. However, what we need to be aware of is that there are possible negative consequences for the talker if we choose to act as a listener in an unsafe way and these include the following:

- If we direct or lead the conversation

- If we judge or evaluate what someone's saying
- If we blame
- If we get aggressive
- If we moralise or preach
- If we advise or teach
- If we don't accept another's feelings
- If we inappropriately talk about ourselves
- If we interrogate
- If we reassure and humour
- If we label and diagnose
- If we over-interpret
- If we distract or are irrelevant
- If we fake attention
- If we place time pressures on the talker

I would now like you to rate yourselves against each of the fifteen non listening behaviours listed. I would like you to rate yourselves on a scale of 0 – 10 - 0 being never, 5 being quite often, 10 being all the time. Then, think about how much, for example, you direct and lead the conversation or you judge and evaluate others when you are having a conversation.

This is really important, as a self-reflection activity because if you are going to be a person that others regard as being safe to talk to then you do need to be aware, all the time, of the ways in which you are actually listening to others. It is important not to beat ourselves around the head about this in the sense that there are always times when we are more pressured, or more stressed and when listening is harder. As long as we are aware of that and as long as we are aware that at those times we need to be even more vigilant about monitoring our own behaviours, then I think we can be more successful in this area.

Activity 5

Understanding another's world - getting inside their frame of reference

There are different levels of understanding another person's world. When we first meet someone we have very little opportunity to understand his or her frame of reference. However, if we are truly safe people with whom to talk and we tend not to have too many preconceptions about others, then, through time, we will develop a much more secure and deeper understanding of their world. It's this kind of information that is helpful when we are trying to put what they are saying into context. What our relationships need to be based upon overall is a sense of mutual understanding in which each of our worlds is both acknowledged and appreciated. I think this goes for our relationships with children, students, parents and one another and this is certainly not some kind of soft, touchy feely, conception. This is something much more practical, much more down to earth and much more authentic.

Good behaviour in any classroom is based upon good relationships and good relationships are based upon good listening. I do need to reinforce, I think, that being a good listener across such a range of relationships isn't always easy because they entail different levels of involvement, roles, emotional styles and expectations. We know that there are sources of interference and we need to be aware of these and we also know that we need to make the choice to work on disciplining our listening and responding in a helpful way to others. We need to look at our so called bad habits of listening and change these and I think that so far in this session we have had some opportunity to consider those and to think about ways in which we need to further develop our skills.

This final exercise involves three activities which are basically repeated with one variation. What you are asked to do here is to use the second person singular in all instances where your partner uses the first person singular. The second exercise is designed to ensure that you have listened and understood before you make your contribution in the conversation. The final exercise asks you to listen carefully so that you can summarise another person's frame of reference. The take home task requires you to actually repeat these exercises as many times as you consider necessary in order to work on these particular aspects of your listening skills. You can do this with another partner in the home context.

Activity 5a

In this paired exercise, person A will talk about himself or herself for three to five minutes and pause after each sentence so as to allow Person B to respond. Person B's task here is to repeat everything that person A says but to switch all of the first person singular into second person singular. For example, 'I feel' becomes 'you feel'. I would suggest that you start with very brief sentences before moving on to longer ones as this will be easier. After this first part of the exercise I would like you to discuss your reactions to what transpired and then reverse roles.

Activity 5b

This is another paired exercise in which you are going to be asked to check out another's frame of reference. What I would like you to do here is to hold a conversation with your partner in which each of you talks in very brief sentences. Each of the sentences is repeated by the person who is listening using the second instead of the first person singular. Listeners can only become active talkers by adding something new to the conversation after they have checked out through repetition that they heard accurately the last sentence spoken. So if the talker doesn't consider the listener has been sufficiently accurate, then he or she must make some kind of sign to indicate this by either clicking their fingers or raising their right hand. If the listener cannot correct the accuracy of their response on their own, the speaker helps them out before continuing the exercise. Once this activity is completed both partners should discuss their thoughts and feelings about what has transpired in this exercise.

Activity 5c

This again is a paired exercise where you listen whilst your partner talks to you either about how he/she feels about his relationship skills or some area in which he/she is interested. When your partner is talking you may use bodily communication but not talk yourself. At the end of two minutes you have to summarise what your partner has been saying from his/her frame of reference. This includes using the first person singular. You can also move into his/her chair as you do this. It may be helpful if we make use of an audio cassette for checking on accuracy afterwards and also, I think, for really self-reflecting on individual skills and areas that we may wish to develop further in the future. This is a supportive exercise intended to help us to develop our skills in this particular area and to begin to become what I would call emotionally literate and disciplined listeners.

True or False?

1. Children are taught when they're little to be good listeners.

2. People's thinking can interfere with the way they listen.

3. Listening is an entirely natural activity.

4. If you are able to listen to others then you should be able to listen to yourself.

5. People can sometimes resist listening to other people who blame and get angry with them.

6. You never have to be self-disciplined to be a good listener.

7. People are far more likely to talk to others with whom they feel secure and safe than with those whom they don't.

8. It is always up to the individual person to communicate exactly what they want.

9. People who have something that they can't wait to say generally listen well.

10. Some people listen too much simply because they are afraid of disclosing anything about themselves.

11. An important aspect in developing trust is to be able to listen and then keep someone else's confidences or secrets.

Module 2 – Activity 2

<table>
<tr><td>

**Barriers to Listening
Discussion Points**

</td></tr>
</table>

1. Try and write down or discuss as many of the intentional barriers and filters that you have experienced when attempting to listen to others. So anything that has interfered with your listening is an intentional barrier or filter.

2. Can you discuss a time when your own or another person's emotions have interfered with your capacity to listen. Can you give examples?

3. Are there certain types or categories of people to whom you find it difficult to listen? Can you describe them and why this may be the case.

4. Are there any words, phrases or attitudes from others that tend to trigger off in your resistance to listening? Can you describe them?

5. Are there any particular areas or topics which you find it difficult to listen to?

6. Are there any other sources of interference that you have experienced with your listening?

Module 2 – Activity 3

Being a Good or Bad Listener

1. Think of at least three individuals in your current or past life that you would regard as being really good at listening and three that you consider to be very poor at listening.

   1. ....
   2. ....
   3. ....

2. Then I would like you to write down on one half of the sheet of A4 paper all the characteristics you had associated with a good listener and then on the other side of the page all of those that you had associated with a bad listener.

Good Listener Characteristics	Bad Listener Characteristics

3. Now have a short period of self-reflection assessing your own skills, resources and deficits as a listener looking at these two lists which ones would apply to you and which ones do you think you could change and what do you need to do in order to make such changes.

Module 2 – Activity 4

Self-Reflection Activity

> ### Unsafe Listening –
> ### Are you a 'safe' listener?

Do you?

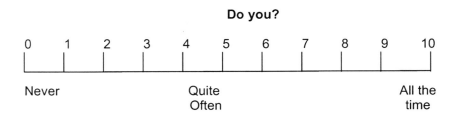

Rate yourself against each of the unsafe listening skills below:

Direct or lead the conversation
Judge or evaluate what someone's saying
Blame
Get aggressive
Moralise or preach
Advise or teach
Don't accept another's feelings
Inappropriately talk about ourselves
Interrogate
Reassure and humour
Label and diagnose
Over-interpret
Distract or are irrelevant
Fake attention
Place time pressures on the talker

Emotionally Literate Behaviour Management

MODULE 3

Defining and Asserting Yourself

EMOTIONALLY LITERATE BEHAVIOUR MANAGEMENT

MODULE 3 – DEFINING AND ASSERTING YOURSELF

Introduction

If we are going to be able to assert ourselves in our relationships then we do need to be in touch with our own feelings. It is important to recognise that the way that we sometimes think, both professionally and personally, can interfere with our ability to be assertive. I think that in all our relationships, we constantly make the sorts of choices that create and define ourselves, both to ourselves and to others. How we do this can be either negative or positive and usually includes the way that we talk about ourselves, the way that we start and maintain relationships, the way that we assert ourselves, listen and manage our feelings and work effectively on the conflicts that we encounter on a daily basis. In the same way that we can't avoid actually communicating with others, we can also not avoid making the kinds of choices that define ourselves.

Being able to assert ourselves is probably one of the most important parts of defining ourselves in relationships. Without developing this ability we are, in effect, losing control both internally and externally within both the school and the social context. This includes being able to initiate relationships and talk about ourselves openly. In psychological terms, I'd suggest that being assertive can be defined as the capacity to express our wants and feelings and to stand up for ourselves without unnecessarily violating others' needs. We need to acknowledge our own thoughts and feelings in this process. This is important because very often there is a risk in being assertive that we can be out of touch with our own true feelings and rather than asserting what's really us, we may be asserting a view of ourselves which is based on the internalisation of others' thoughts and feelings, e.g. those of our parents or those that brought us up.

We also need to think realistically and be careful to avoid the kinds of negative thinking that can inhibit our assertiveness, e.g. thoughts related to gender – that men are unable to show affection as much as women or that women are unable to stand up for their own rights as effectively as men. We need to be able to talk about ourselves and communicate our needs and wants and we also need to be able to be positive to others, both in words and actions and do this with an absence of defensiveness. So we need to feel secure enough to own up to our own mistakes and avoid blaming others for our troubles and problems. This is a tall order. However, if we can begin to develop a climate like this both within ourselves and within the staff room, then I think this also filters out into the classroom context and we begin to have a less blaming and more open and mutually respective classroom context.

We also need to be able to stand up for ourselves, sharing negative thoughts and feelings about others and setting limits and not saying 'yes' when we actually mean 'no'. We need to be able to use the right amount of strength, having enough respect for ourselves and the other person so that we know how much or how far we can push a situation when we are asserting ourselves. It is also important that we know our own limits and those of others so that we can be realistic in choosing when to be assertive and when, for example, to pull back slightly, e.g. in situations where the risks may outweigh the gains. In this first activity, which is entitled, 'Self Assessment Scaling Activity, I'd like you to read through each of the statements and then rate yourselves on a scale of 0-10 as to how you feel you consider your skills are in each of the following areas of defining and asserting yourself. (0 would be very weak, 5 would be average, and 10 would be excellent). The areas are as follows:

1. You are aware of your feelings and aspirations.
2. You are free from unrealistic thoughts that mitigate against self-definition and assertion.
3. You are able to engage in a speech that is helpful rather than negative.
4. You can develop and maintain intimate relationships through appropriately revealing personal information.
5. You are able to admit to weaknesses or vulnerabilities and strengths.
6. You are able to appropriately touch and be touched.
7. You can express your wants and needs clearly.
8. You can put away constricting limits and say 'yes'.
9. You can take initiative.
10. You can express positive thoughts and feelings to others and about them.
11. You can act positively towards others.
12. You can own up to making mistakes and avoid defensive responses.
13. You can express negative thoughts and feelings towards others.
14. You can say 'no' and set your own limits.
15. You can end a relationship in an appropriately positive manner.
16. You can avoid colluding and others' attempts to have you behave in a way that does not sit comfortably with your true self and merely meets their own needs.
17. You can assert yourself to an appropriate extent in the right situation.
18. You can avoid being unnecessarily negative or destructive about someone.
19. You can handle other people's feedback and criticism in an appropriately assertive way.
20. You know when you can't or shouldn't assert yourself.

It will then be helpful for each of you to independently make up your own lists of skills that you'd like to further develop and to share these via the discussion process in this Module.

Activity 2

What we sometimes disregard (because we think we already know) it is what it actually 'looks' like in terms of bodily and vocal messages when we are being assertive. We can tend to have some very stock or stereotypical views as to how someone should sound and look like. So, as a means of perhaps clarifying these bodily and vocal components, I'd like you to thought storm in smaller groups as to what the following would look like, or sound like, or be like if they were describing someone who was being assertive. The headings are as follows:

Eye contact
Facial expression
Body posture
Gesture
Proximity
Absence of negative bodily communication
Absence of distracting bodily communication
Vocal messages -volume, tone, speed, and inflection

I'll give you an example for the last one on the list - inflection. I would suggest that assertive behaviours would include the presence of inflections that emphasise assertion and the absence of inflections that indicate aggression and are considered to be put-downs.

Activity 3

Why can't I be assertive?

Very often I think that what stops us from being assertive and asserting ourselves are our own mental barriers that we have either created ourselves or those created for us by others. We may have subconsciously absorbed them throughout the years or as we have developed in terms of personality and social skills. I think these include demands that we make on ourselves, fears about others' reactions to us and fears about our reactions to others' reactions. For example, I may be continually saying to myself, 'I must be nice', 'I must avoid conflict', 'I must be liked by people', 'I must not be selfish', I must not hurt other people', 'I mustn't show anger', I must not admit to making a mistake ', 'I must not take a risk', etc, etc. We may be fearful of others' reactions. We may be frightened that others might reject us, criticise us or consider us emotional or over-emotional or pushy, etc. We may think that we cannot do certain things such as handle rejection or handle conflict or handle uncertainty, etc. In this activity I'd like you to think about any mental barriers that you may have to asserting yourself in both the school and the home context. I'd like you to relate to specific situations in your own relationships and consider the following headings:

Demands on yourself
Fears about others' reactions
Your fears about your reactions to others' reactions

I'd like you to really try and think now about the unrealistic thoughts that are most applicable to you and to try and reformulate some of these perhaps into more realistic thoughts. It may be helpful to do this in smaller group contexts and then for each group to feed back via a plenary and discussion session at the end of this activity.

Activity 4

Very often we'll run into difficulties in our relationships when we have been unable to be positive about what we want or wish for and we feel that we can't take the initiative. This kind of absence of positive behaviour tends to create an emotional climate in which negative behaviours occur or are more likely to occur since one or both of the individuals involved feels that they are being inadequately listened to. This is something that we know from our session on becoming a good listener. When we don't feel listened to we tend to either withdraw or become aggressive or retreat into ourselves. We can also become angry and uncooperative. This is true of relationships which are both intensely personal, e.g. with our partners or loved ones or relationships which are less emotionally based but however are still very important or significant to us. When we can be positive we can help to prevent other people's negative behaviours. I think it is just actually a matter of common sense that expressing liking and being positive towards others in a relationship, tends to increase the likelihood of their behaviour being the same towards you: they'll mirror what you actually show them, they'll reflect it back to you.

However, part of being positive, I think, is being able to talk positively and being able to express your wants and wishes in an assertive way. I think this can be done by using 'I' statements. For example, I may wish my husband to be more affectionate towards me and if I was going to request this in an inhibited way, I may say to him, 'You do love me don't you? If I was going to be aggressive about it, I'd accuse him of probably always thinking of himself first and not considering me at all and getting quite angry about it and perhaps suggesting that he doesn't know how to make someone of the opposite sex feel happy or loved or wanted. However, if I was going to be assertive – I'd actually feed him with a very sensible 'I' message which positively reflects the behaviours that I want him to show towards me. For example, 'I really like it when you give me a big hug and show how much you love me. It's something I really want. It's important to me'.

These are also the kinds of messages that we need to use in the classroom. 'I really appreciate it when you sit down and do your work like that. It really makes me feel good and makes me feel proud of you as well'. In this next activity, I'd like you to think about a recent situation in your own relationships – any of them - could be with your partner or a sibling or a child, in which you responded in the following ways:

Firstly, where you have been inhibited in expressing what you wanted.
Secondly, where you have been aggressive.
Thirdly, where you have been assertive in expressing your wants and needs.

Next consider how you would have chosen to behave differently so that you could have been assertive in the two situations in which you were inhibited and aggressive. What could you have done differently? How could you have responded differently? What could have ensured a more positive outcome for you?
It would be really helpful if you could discuss these responses in pairs and then feedback to the group as a whole.

Activity 5

Personal Responsibility

I think it is possible to look at life in terms of it being some kind of contest between maintaining our view of ourselves and being assertive about who we are and what we want and also coping with others who will generally try to impose their behaviour and their definitions of situations on us. I think we all have pictures of ourselves which imply not only how we relate to others but also how we think others should relate to us. What we really need to do in terms of defining ourselves, is to make sure we have the courage to stand up to other people's negative behaviour and to their attempts to label us or define us in their own terms rather than those that we would want. This really is what Richard Nelson Jones terms a personal responsibility view of assertion – one that entails a number of choices. In coping with others' negative behaviour, we do need to make choices about what our own contribution is, e.g. to create a negative situation. Sometimes it's too easy to attribute the responsibility for negative events outside of ourselves. i.e. blaming others or the context rather than developing our own locus of control. We also need to question how defensive we are actually being. When the view of ourself is being threatened, it's tempting to battle back at somebody under the guise or pretence of assertion whereas in actual fact what we are really doing is finding it difficult to take feedback on an aspect of our behaviour and the other person may have a point.

However, when strong emotions are involved, when someone is perhaps criticising an emotional aspect of our being, it is very much harder to cope with this than it is to take on board something new in the area of cognitive learning. Also we need to think about the question: 'Is it worth actually being assertive?' We need to know whether we have got sufficient involvement or we have bought into something to the extent that we wish to really choose to be assertive. Sometimes, if someone else is highly threatened by us and would potentially become destructive if challenged, is it worth being assertive in that particular situation?

And also, finally, we need to think about whether we do or do not have the requisite skills. There are probably six areas in which we need to build up our skills. We need to be aware; we need to overcome our mental barriers; we need to manage our anxiety effectively; we need to know what to say, i.e. using positive 'I' statements; we need to know how to say it, so being assertive and avoiding non-assertive vocal and bodily communication and we need to act appropriately if necessary, backing up our words with actions. What we need to be able to do is to avoid the 'you' blame assertions and statements and to develop the 'I' rational statements. In 'I' rational statements people generally state how they feel and why they feel that way in a calm and rational fashion. 'You' blame statements engender defensiveness and usually involve accusatory statements which include putting down other people.

We appear to have three ways of coping with negative behaviours: that's the inhibited aggressive and assertive responses we talked about earlier. So just a quick reminder of those – an example could be that someone was late to a dinner party you were organising (at least an hour late and they hadn't contacted you to let you know they were going to be late). An inhibited response would be for you to say, 'Oh, its okay, it's nice to see you, don't worry'. An aggressive response may be you actually swearing at them and telling them that the dinner is spoiled now. An assertive response would involve you in utilising an 'I' rational assertive statement such as: 'I'm extremely upset at you being so late because you didn't contact me. Was there a reason for it?' The activity here requires you to formulate what you would consider to be inhibited, assertive and aggressive responses to three situations that I'm going to briefly outline for you. Work together in groups to formulate these responses then we will feed back at the end of ten minutes or so working time. The situations are as follows:

1. New neighbours have moved into the street and continually play their music very loud into the night, sometimes until 4 or 5 o'clock into the morning. Recently they've taken to doing this on a Sunday. You are extremely upset about this because you have to get up for work in the morning.

2. Someone on your staff team is continually taking credit for work that you've actually done and not acknowledging the input that you've had into the group tasks. You are getting fed up with this.

3. One of the parents that you have had to deal with recently has been quite offensive in an overtly sexual way towards you and you feel quite threatened by these overtures that he/she has made and need to make some response.

Activity 6

Avoiding Collusion

This is probably one of the most significant things that we need to do if we are going to successfully develop our ability to assert ourselves and to ultimately protect our mental and emotional health within a range of contexts. People frequently use a variety of behaviours in order to get what they want, e.g. someone may use anger as a means of getting their own way; someone may avoid dealing with the issue directly by obscuring it; another person may find that bursting into tears is an effective means of getting others to do what she/he wants whilst another person may withdraw their affection for others if they don't give the kind of feed back that they want. People tend to use a variety of devices in order to get what they want and generally this can be at somebody else's expense.

It is important for you to be aware when these things are happening so that you can actually respond to them in an assertive way. This will ensure that you don't get damaged and you avoid the kinds of manipulation that others can display and avoid indulging in these behaviours yourself. What we don't want to do is to collude and allow others to succeed in this kind of manipulation or control technique. Being aware that others are attempting to manipulate you and to define you in this way is the first step in being able to handle their propensity to control you.

We always have three choices. We can either be submissive and actually allow them to maintain false definitions and manipulations, or we can be aggressive and perhaps escalate the situation and the emotional temperature of the situation. Alternatively, and I think perhaps best, we can be assertive by quickly persisting and articulating our own definition of ourself and/or the situation as we see it. Obviously, when someone is highly manipulative then there may be a fourth option that we need to consider which is to actually just simply move away and get out of that relationship or situation. Having the courage to be ourselves also involves us having the courage not to collude with others' views of us and be manipulated by them. It is something that we all need to develop if we are to maintain our own level of mental health and if we are to be able to nurture and support each other in doing the jobs that we do which are emotionally laboursome on a daily basis.

This final activity (which you may want to do as a take-home task), is to list as many ways you can think of in which others that you know have manipulated you. This manipulation may be taking place now or may have taken place in the past. What is important here is for you to actually be able to record the ways in which others have attempted to define you on their terms and the way in which you felt that you had to act according to their wishes although this was against your own feelings and instincts.

Next you can select one or two situations and write out a plan of action for each one in which you decide how you would stop colluding in their behaviours and begin to handle the situation assertively. This outline needs to identify what's going on, what your responses currently are, what this is eventually leading to and how you think you can change your behaviours and responses and become more assertive in order to gain the best or a better outcome for yourself.

Then discuss this in pairs and feedback to the group as a whole. I think it would be very interesting to see how our definitions of assertiveness have developed alongside the ways in which we can all begin to think about further developing our skills in this area.

I would finally leave you with the thought that the emotionally literate school is one in which people can and do behave in an assertive way. Where they can't behave in this way is when they'll continually encounter defensiveness, resistance and negative feedback in response to any kind of positive or assertive behaviours. That is exactly what we don't want.

What we do want is to create a climate in which people can be in touch with their own feelings and where they can also be realistic about the demands that they make on themselves and upon each other. When people can act in this assertive manner and communicate their wishes and wants clearly and take initiatives, there will be generally a climate in which people can be seen to be making the effort to be likeable and to express their liking of others to them. In effect the end result would be an emotional climate in which people can feel free and happy to be constructive and to be positive human beings. That is exactly what we want, not just for the students that we teach but for ourselves and it needs to start, as I've said before, with us.

Module 3 – Activity 5

Inhibited, Assertive and Aggressive Responses

1. New neighbours have moved into the street and continually play their music very loud into the night, sometimes until 4 or 5 o'clock into the morning. Recently they've taken to doing this on a Sunday. You are extremely upset about this because you have to get up for work in the morning.

2. Someone on your staff team is continually taking credit for work that you've actually done and not acknowledging the input that you've had into the group tasks. You are getting fed up with this.

3. One of the parents that you have had to deal with recently has been quite offensive in an overtly sexual way towards you and you feel quite threatened by these overtures that he/she has made and need to make some response.

Module 3 – Activity 6

Self-Assessment Scaling Activity

Read through each of the statement and then rate yourselves on a scale of 0-10 as to how you feel you consider your skills are in each of the following areas of defining and asserting yourself. (0 would be very weak, 5 would be average, and 10 would be excellent.) The areas are as follows:

1. You are aware of your feelings and aspirations.

```
0    1    2    3    4    5    6    7    8    9    10
```

2. Your are free from unrealistic thoughts that mitigate against self-definition and assertion.

```
0    1    2    3    4    5    6    7    8    9    10
```

3. You are able to engage in a speech that is helpful rather than negative.

```
0    1    2    3    4    5    6    7    8    9    10
```

4. You can develop and maintain intimate friendships through appropriately revealing personal information.

```
0    1    2    3    4    5    6    7    8    9    10
```

5. Your are able to admit to weaknesses or vulnerabilities and strengths.

```
0    1    2    3    4    5    6    7    8    9    10
```

6. You are able to appropriately touch and be touched.

```
0    1    2    3    4    5    6    7    8    9    10
```

7. You can express your wants and needs clearly.

```
0    1    2    3    4    5    6    7    8    9    10
```

Self-Assessment Scaling Activity

8. You can put away constricting limits and say "yes".

   0   1   2   3   4   5   6   7   8   9   10

9. You can take initiative.

   0   1   2   3   4   5   6   7   8   9   10

10. You can express positive thoughts and feelings to others and about them.

    0   1   2   3   4   5   6   7   8   9   10

11. You can act positively towards others.

    0   1   2   3   4   5   6   7   8   9   10

12. You can own up to making mistakes and avoid defensive responses.

    0   1   2   3   4   5   6   7   8   9   10

13. You can express negative thoughts and feelings towards others.

    0   1   2   3   4   5   6   7   8   9   10

14. You can say "no" and set your own limits.

    0   1   2   3   4   5   6   7   8   9   10

15. You can end a relationship in an appropriately positive manner.

    0   1   2   3   4   5   6   7   8   9   10

Self-Assessment Scaling Activity

16. You can avoid colluding and others' attempts to have you behave in a way that does not sit comfortably with your true self and merely meets their own needs.

0   1   2   3   4   5   6   7   8   9   10

17. You can assert yourself to an appropriate extent in the right situation.

0   1   2   3   4   5   6   7   8   9   10

18. You can avoid being unnecessarily negative or destructive about someone.

0   1   2   3   4   5   6   7   8   9   10

19. You can handle other people's feedback and criticism in appropriate assertive way.

0   1   2   3   4   5   6   7   8   9   10

20. You know when you can't or shouldn't assert yourself.

0   1   2   3   4   5   6   7   8   9   10

Emotionally Literate Behaviour Management

MODULE 4

Managing Stress and Anger

EMOTIONALLY LITERATE BEHAVIOUR MANAGEMENT

MODULE 4 –MANAGING STRESS AND ANGER

Introduction

We have previously talked about how we need to be able to identify and label our own feelings and express them to one another in an appropriately assertive way, whilst also being able to listen to both the words and feelings of others. Clearly, these are the kinds of skills that we want to develop if we are to be considered emotionally literate teachers and individuals. Another key element of emotional literacy, however, is the ability to regulate or manage or feelings and, in particular, anger and the stresses which are often related to or emanate from our angry feelings.

The major emphasis within this Module therefore, is on the choices we can make in disciplining our thinking so that we can regulate our feelings, particularly those that are negative for both ourselves and for others around us. I think this is a key goal for all of us, both in our professional and our personal lives as we are far more likely to be able to act in a way that effectively allows us to reach our goals if we develop these skills. I think that we are likely to be most effective in our relationships when we assume responsibility for the way that we think, feel and act. Assuming responsibility for our feelings involves us in learning how to express them where appropriate and also how to regulate them when we need to do so. What we need to be able to do is to attribute responsibility for what happens in our life. We need to continually take responsibility for acknowledging managing our feelings if we are to maintain any appropriate level of mental wellbeing and physical wellbeing.

We must not avoid assuming personal responsibility for managing our anger and our stresses. This is essential. There are many ways in which we can avoid taking this responsibility and these include denial, protection, and misattributing responsibility i.e. an over-emphasis on making others responsible for how we feel. We can collude in situations that we don't like by not being assertive. We can enlist collusions of others. We can engage in power playing or we can engage in rationalisation, i.e. deceiving ourselves and others by justifying feelings unjustifiably. We can avoid difficult people or situations. We can block off or defend ourselves against positive qualities or against showing these for others. We can distort situations so as to maintain our pictures of ourselves and we can misuse language, e.g. using expressions such as, 'they did it to me', 'it just happened', rather than actually using 'I' statements and maintaining a locus of control as we discussed earlier in Module 3.

Activity 1

Responsibility and choice

The following are two descriptions of situations which I would like you to read through and then consider your views via group discussion.

Situation 1 - Jane is extremely angry with her Head teacher whom she perceives to be very aggressive and bullying. She has recently had an altercation with her in which she suggested that she felt unfairly treated. Jane attempted to be assertive and tell her that her behaviours were aggressive and bullying when they had 1:1 meetings and that she found her expectations unrealistic as regards to what work outcomes were expected of her. Her Head teacher then stated that she felt that Jane was actually highly inefficient herself and also indulged in disparaging her to others on the staff team. Jane's morale is at an extremely low ebb and colleagues are now beginning to avoid her as she is making them feel depressed when she moans about the Head teacher. Jane's resentment and anger against the Head teacher is extremely virulent.

Situation 2 – Alex feels in a consent tense state and is extremely stressed. She is the kind of person who doesn't need to sleep very much usually and tends to work all the hours God sends but she feels that not to do so would be to show weakness and laziness. She also expects the same high standards in terms of work commitment from her peers and disparages those who don't seem to meet with her requirements or who suggest that they have other priorities in their lives such as family or social lives. Recently she has been extremely had tempered and sleeping even less than she had previously. She has also lost her appetite and her relationships with workmates have deteriorated. She smokes, is overweight and takes little exercise and is beginning to feel very lethargic, particularly in the early afternoons.

What I'd like you to do here is to consider your views on the following:

- First of all, the extent to which the main character is avoiding personal responsibility for managing her feelings.
- Secondly, what you think the unrealistic thoughts might be that she has which are contributing to her feeling so strongly and,
- Thirdly, what kinds of choices might the individual make that would perhaps aid her in managing the feelings she has more effectively? It would be helpful if we could do this in pairs or smaller groups and then feedback to the group as a whole.

Activity 2

Exploring your anger

Anger is clearly a complex emotion, e.g. it gets combined with others such as hurt, jealousy, fear, powerlessness, guilt, frustration and depression. It can often be seen as a secondary emotion to these and there are also many variations in the ways and extents to which it is acknowledged and expressed. It may be denied altogether or compensated for by positive behaviour or the anger may be projected onto others. It may also be manifested in aggressive put-downs or even bodily harm towards others and can lead to or contribute to depression. Raymond Novaco sees anger as an emotional response to provocation involving thoughts, feelings and behaviour and considers angry feelings to be primed 'and exacerbated by tension, agitation and ill humour'. In his view, chronic anger and proneness to provocation may have serious implications for relationships. Just pause to consider the times we have all spent looking at so-called angry children – those that we have labelled as being angry and frustrated because they seem unable to develop the kinds of self-management skills that we deem to be appropriate if people are to be considered socially acceptable. However, I think that what we'd all accept, is that alongside the notions of responsibility and choice, there is also an element of all of us being provided with opportunities to learn skills of self-management which will enable us to cope more effectively. As teachers and professionals or those caring for young people, we certainly need to display these skills ourselves given that we are models for these students and in a very powerful position in terms of being able to teach and instil appropriate behaviours and self management skills in those we support and care for on a daily basis.

There are many reasons why we get angry and I'm sure that if we did a quick thought now, we'd come up with a very similar list to that that a group of teenagers would also produce or a group of 7 or 8 year olds. The language would be different but there would be similar items on the list: people putting us down, people swearing at us, people being aggressive towards us, people making us feel stupid or silly or unintelligent, people blaming us for things that weren't our fault, people undermining us, people abusing us, etc. It is very important for us all to explore the role of anger in our own lives. To what extent is this a problem for us and how do we choose to show anger ourselves? What are the positive and negative consequences of our behaviours or displays of anger and how do we react and cope when others get angry with us and express their anger towards us? These are all important issues. Consequently, I'd like you to consider the following eleven questions on an individual basis prior to discussing your responses with a partner and then feeding back to the whole group.

1. To what extent do you think of yourself as an angry person?
2. To what extent is your anger a problem for you or others?
3. What situations make you feel angry?
4. What people make you feel angry?
5. Can you list the physical reactions you experience when you get angry?
6. Can you list the thoughts that you have about other people when you get angry?
7. Can you list the thoughts that you have about yourself when you get angry?
8. What is it you actually do, i.e. how do you behave when you are angry?
9. Are there any positive consequences for yourself or others which come from your anger?
10. What are the negative consequences for yourself or others that come from your anger?
11. How do you feel, physically react and then behave when other people get angry with you?

Activity 3

Realistic self-rules

One important way of managing anger in relationships is to express it assertively. Once again, the importance of making positive 'I' statements needs to be emphasised here. However, although this may be valuable it may not be sufficient in all cases. We need to take responsibility for angry feelings and this doesn't just involve acknowledging and expressing them but also means that we need to be more aware of how we may be contributing to generating and sustaining our anger.

When we feel angry it's very often all too easy to just see others' provocative behaviours as a problem - it's their fault, they made me do it, they upset me, they made it worse. When we begin to really self-reflect and analyse, we can often see that we do have more choices about how we think, feel and act, than we are possibly aware of at that moment in time. What I'm asking you to do in this activity is to begin to explore how you can change some of the ways in which you yourselves contribute to your anger.

Richard Nelson Jones introduces an ATF framework in which anger can be viewed as follows: A standing for the event or the provocation, T for your thoughts, F for your feelings. He thinks that the realism of your own internal rules or standards is very important to the effectiveness of your thinking. What you think is vital in terms of positively influencing your feelings. These can be altered if your thoughts are more realistic. Realistic inner rules tend to be based on your own needs and values and have a degree of flexibility, i.e. being open to change. Realistic inner rules also allow you to be clear and realistic about your resources, acknowledging your own strengths and have an emphasis on coping with situations rather than being a perfectionist, and they are also more conducive to minimising negative emotions. The key here, when we are angry, is not to react impulsively but to stop and think and make more measured approaches to a situation. It is essential that we develop realistic internal rules and I'd like you now to participate in this activity which asks you to think of one or more recent situations in your life where you felt angry and for each one to record the following:

- The activating event or the thing that provoked you.
- Your thoughts and particularly focusing on unrealistic internal rules.
- Your feelings.
- A reformulation of the unrealistic into realistic internal rules.
- Any changes in your feelings and actions that may result from your more realistic internal rules.

It may be helpful to record these reformulated rules and play them back to yourself in order to reinforce these new patterns of behaviour and responses. It would also be helpful to share these responses with a partner and discuss the difficulty or otherwise of being able to reformulate unrealistic internal rules into realistic ones.

Activity 4

Being assertive

We know that feelings of anger generally tend to be associated with feelings of powerlessness and having to put up with and cope with other people's negative behaviours towards us. We also know, that being more assertive helps us both prevent and handle anger-engendering situations. However, we make things worse for ourselves and we do it again and again if we fall into the traps of not saying what we want, nor speaking out for ourselves, not setting realistic limits and also by colluding in other people's power play.

These are all the kinds of things that we have got to avoid - six possible areas as follows. The first one is being aware when you have got the choice of responding in an assertive manner, secondly, overcoming mental barriers to assertion, thirdly managing anxiety more appropriately, fourthly knowing what to say verbally including the use of positive 'I' statements, fifth, knowing how to say it including using assertive vocal and bodily communications systems and finally, sixth, acting appropriately, and, if necessary, backing up your words with actions.

It is always important that we focus on choosing our behaviours and being very clear about choosing assertive behaviours as opposed to aggressive or inhibited responses. We need to remember at all times that either intentionally or unintentionally we may be choosing to sustain situations that cause us to feel anger or unhappiness. We also need to consider whether it is possible to manage our angry feelings by making different or better choices and by being more assertive.

In this next activity I'd like you to just work in pairs and think of an important situation in your own relationships where your lack of assertion may be contributing to you feeling angry. Then consider and perhaps write out first of all the risks and gains from acting more assertively in this situation, how you might behave more assertively and how you might cope with any resistance or negative feedback that you might get as a direct result of your being assertive in this situation. Then I'd like you to have a go at practising your assertion skills in a real life situation i.e. acting out via a role play situation. Have a go at talking through these situations and perhaps coaching one another into developing a more appropriately assertive response to a typical situation that you are currently encountering.

Activity 5

Handling criticism

For most of us, particularly in a professional situation, one of the hardest things to handle is criticism. However, we need to focus on the fact that we have got a choice both in how we perceive and in how we react to criticism. What is important is to recognise and deal appropriately with negative criticism. This is vital if we are to create a staff team which is truly emotionally literate and able to respond effectively to each other in times of crisis and problem situations – one where teachers can actually walk into each others classrooms and feel that they can say, 'I've found this difficult' and 'I don't feel that you have supported me in this, your criticism of me was unfair, unjust', etc, etc. We need to be able to have the conversations where we are truly authentic and open with each other so that we can begin to respond effectively to criticism and we combat and mitigate against negative criticism within the learning context. Negative and critical teachers equals negative and critical students.

In this activity I'd like you to work independently in the first instance and to write down how you see yourself feeling, thinking and acting when you are criticised. I'd like to give some specific examples if you can. Then consider which of the following skills might help you to handle criticism more effectively in future situations which are similar to those you've described earlier:

- Assessing whether the criticism is actually worth getting stewed up about.
- Counting to 10, 20 or 100.
- Regulating your breathing.
- Withdrawing in order to make your point at a later date.
- Responding in a very reflective manner.
- Gathering more information.
- Clearing up any misunderstandings or misperceptions or conceptions.
- Being assertive – whether that's in agreeing, apologising or assertively disagreeing.
- Making use of task-orientated inner speech, e.g. keep calm and remember what I want to achieve in this situation.
- Stick to the issues and avoid put-downs, etc.
- Exploring the rightness and appropriateness of your own position.
- Attempting to problem-solve and reappraise the situation in a step-by-step constructive manner.
- Managing the conflict.

Next discuss in pairs your responses and this concept of choice in relation to coping with negative criticism. I'd also then like to focus on the kinds of skills that the majority of us would like to develop and to consider the possibility of further work in this area.

Activity 6

Managing stress

Finally in this session we can consider the nature of stress and the possible relationships between anger and stress. We know that if we are under stress at work or at home then we are likely to be more irritable or likely to lose our tempers. This may contribute to relationship deterioration which can also then become an additional stress. Continuous inability to actually express anger or get anger out may also be stressful and our body may begin to show signs of this stress via headaches, ulcers, lack of sleep, etc.

We know that stress is person-specific and we know that each of us has an optimum level of stress or a level at which stress becomes too much for us to cope with and remain effective in the work or social spheres. As an initial activity here, I'd like us just to thought storm what we think the main stresses are that we would experience, particularly in the school situation, and then perhaps to rank those together in order of which ones we feel would be most significant or most likely to occur for the majority of us in this context.

Finally, we can consider the ways in which we can handle some of these stresses and which you, personally, may wish to utilise in order to help yourself manage the stresses that you are currently experiencing. I'd like you to consider one of the main stressors that you are currently experiencing and to then tick against this list of self-help interventions which you think might help you to manage this stress. Also, give a reason why you have chosen each of the items on the list. These are as follows:

- Attributing responsibility accurately.
- To listen to your body.
- To talk more about yourself and how you feel.
- To develop a support network.
- To be more assertive.
- To become a better and more effective listener.
- To learn to manage your anger more effectively.
- To develop managing conflict skills.
- To develop more realistic internal rules for yourself.
- To anticipate the future in a more realistic sense.
- To learn how to break bigger tasks into smaller, more achievable, steps.
- To become more skilled at generating alternative solutions to difficulties and problems.
- To develop a range of recreational outlets.
- To learn relaxation techniques and strategies.
- To be more positive in participating about your health.
- To develop an individual plan for implementing one or more of these self-help interventions for managing your particular stresses and associated angry feelings.

It may be helpful to take this activity home and spend some time reflecting upon the kind of self-help interventions that you could, or can, or will use in the future and to discuss these with the people who are significant to you in your life. It may well be the case that they are contributing, or you are contributing to maintaining certain stressful situations in the home situation which then, of course, impact upon what goes on in school. It think this is a really useful thing to do because ultimately the skill with which we manage feelings of anger and stress are likely to benefit our relationships and good relationships lead to good feelings and positive outcomes.

Conversely, if we don't manage feelings of anger and stress in the right way, then obviously we know that immense harm can be caused both to ourselves and to our relationships with significant others and those in the school and learning context. What we really want to achieve here is a heightened awareness and an increased ability to manage ourselves more effectively. If we can do it, that's when we can model the right behaviours, the right responses, the right choices to the children and students that we are caring for in school. We need to remember at all times that being emotionally literate, being able to cope with our feelings and behaviours and effectively motivate and manage ourselves needs to come first. When we can do this and when we can show that we can do it and support each other in this in the school context, then I think we have got a much better chance of actually instilling and developing these skills in the students that we teach.

Module 4 – Activity 2

1. To what extent do you think of yourself as an angry person?

2. To what extent is your anger a problem for you or others?

3. What situations make you feel angry?

4. What people make you feel angry?

5. Can you list the physical reactions you experience when you get angry?

6. Can you list the thoughts that you have about other people when you get angry?

7. Can you list the thoughts that you have about yourself when you get angry?

8. What is it you actually do, i.e. how do you behave when you are angry?

9. Are there any positive consequences for yourself or others which come from your anger?

10. What are the negative consequences for yourself or others that come from your anger?

11. How do you feel, physically react and then behave when other people get angry with you?

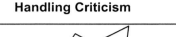

Handling Criticism

Key Skills

Which might help?

- Assessing whether the criticism is actually worth getting stewed up about.

- Counting to 10, 20 or 100.

- Regulating your breathing.

- Withdrawing in order to make your point at a later date.

- Responding in a very reflective manner.

- Gathering more information.

- Clearing up any misunderstandings or misperceptions or conceptions.

- Being assertive – whether that's in agreeing, apologising or assertively disagreeing.

- Making use of task-orientated inner speech, e.g. keep calm and remember what I want to achieve in this situation.

- Stick to the issues and avoid put-downs, etc.

- Exploring the rightness and appropriateness of your own position.

- Attempting to problem-solve and reappraise the situation in a step-by-step constructive manner.

- Managing the conflict.

Managing Stress

Which strategy would help you?

- Attributing responsibility accurately.

- To listen to your body.

- To talk more about yourself and how you feel.

- To develop a support network.

- To be more assertive.

- To become a better and more effective listener.

- To learn to manage your anger more effectively.

- To develop managing conflict skills.

- To develop more realistic internal rules for yourself.

- To anticipate the future in a more realistic sense.

- To learn how to break bigger tasks into smaller, more achievable, steps.

- To become more skilled at generating alternative solutions to difficulties and problems.

- To develop a range of recreational outlets.

- To learn relaxation techniques and strategies.

- To be more positive in participating about your health.

- To develop an individual plan for implementing one or more of these self-help interventions for managing your particular stresses and associated angry feelings.

Emotionally Literate Behaviour Management

MODULE 5

Managing Conflict

EMOTIONALLY LITERATE BEHAVIOUR MANAGEMENT

MODULE 5 – MANAGING CONFLICT

Introduction

Managing conflict involves both sender and receiver skills and actually encompasses most of the skills covered to date in this course. For example, if you have good skills in terms of clearly expressing your needs and desires, you can listen well, you can respond constructively and manage your anger and stress, then clearly there is less likelihood of you getting involved in or participating in unnecessary conflicts. This is something that is very, important given the high stress levels and emotional labour involved in the task of teaching. The last thing that anyone needs, in school community, is to have to encounter or deal with unnecessary conflict on a regular basis.

What we really need to be doing is to ensure that all of us have the kinds of skills necessary to avoid such conflicts or, alternatively, if they do arise, deal with them appropriately and hopefully that's what this module is going to address - actually encouraging all of us to make use of a specific framework for managing conflict effectively. What we will be focusing on in particular is the fact that the essence of a conflict lies in conflicting ideas, interests, wishes and needs.

However, although it is very often not the case, these differences and disagreements need neither be the cause of severe conflict nor of ensuing ill will between individuals. Clearly the negative effects of conflicts don't really need cataloguing and they can cause a great deal of psychological pain to all of us. I think in particular when a work environment such as a school staff room or the whole school context is frequently characterised by destructive conflicts, then the end result is a great deal of stress and unhappiness, high staff turnover, low staff morale – the list could go on and on. However, I would maintain that a degree of conflict is inevitable in work relationships just as it is in personal relationships. Consequently, what we also need to focus on here is the fact that conflict can be for good as well as for ill. It may, at some points, be desirable and can, in fact, be productive rather than destructive.

I would suggest that there are four positive aspects of conflict in relationships which are as follows:

- There could be greater trust when conflicts can build trusts between people who relate despite their differences.
- Increased intimacy so the ability to give and receive honest feedback can be increased.
- Increased self-esteem because partners who are able to manage a conflict effectively may gain in self-esteem simply because they know that their relationship is strong enough to withstand conflict.

- Creative solutions. A course of productive conflict can be viewed as a process of mutual problem solving and I feel that is what it should be viewed as within the context of the workplace in most instances.

Activity 1

In this activity, I would like people to work individually, looking at the list of statements on the sheet and writing down whether or not you consider each statement to be true or false. There are thirty items as follows:

1. Being able to search for mutually acceptable solutions is useful in handling conflicts.

2. Conflicts can result from misunderstandings rather than from genuine differences of interest.

3. Stresses that people experience in their own personal lives can make them prone to engage in destructive conflicts in their relationships.

4. If a conflict continues even though you've really tried to resolve it, you should really feel guilty about it.

5. In order to effectively manage conflict you need to have a very good repertoire of relevant skills.

6. Sometimes the strength of someone's emotions may narrow the scope of their vision within a conflict situation.

7. No-one holds a monopoly on the truth.

8. Tit-for-tat is generally considered fair play.

9. Being able to manage conflicts in a relationship is best viewed as an exercise in joint problem solving for mutual benefit.

10. A conflict can never have a positive outcome.

11. More often than not, people who try to handle conflicts co-operatively are likely to be taken advantage of.

12. In order to win a conflict you need to always compete as hard as possible.

13. Sometimes people can be ruled by their fears when in conflict.

14. In order to manage differences we need to have a clear picture of what these differences actually are.

15. It is often better to avoid differences than face up to them within a relationship.

16. Effective management of conflicts needs people to be able to discipline their thinking appropriately.

17. It pays to act on impulse in a conflict situation.

18. People who tend to carry around a great deal of unfinished business and pain from their relationships with their parents are less inclined to engage in destructive conflicts than those who do not.

19. Conflicts are perhaps best approached in a climate of mutual respect and tolerance.

20. Intimate partners can be capable of changing both themselves and the quality of their relationships.

21. Those who feel that others must be perfect sexual partners place unrealistic expectations on them.

22. Men and women are both psychologically and physically different.

23. People who truly care about their partners and know one another should always be able to sense each other's needs and preferences without having to be told them.

24. Listening appropriately and understanding the other's viewpoint is a useful skill in managing a conflict.

25. People tend to be rational in conflict situations.

26. It's never helpful to express anger when in conflict with another.

27. Don't ever admit to your contribution to sustaining a conflict.

28. It is often helpful to blame the other person in a conflict.

29. A useful way of managing a conflict is to talk about it with third parties rather than with the person directly involved.

30. The less aggressive people are during conflicts, the more likely they are to achieve a desirable outcome.

Answers:
1. True
2. True
3. True
4. False
5. True
6. True
7. True
8. False
9. True
10. False
11. False
12. False
13. True
14. True
15. False
16. True
17. False
18. False
19. True
20. True
21. True
22. False
23. False
24. True
25. False
26. False
27. False
28. False

29. False
30. True

Activity 2

Your skills and deficits in managing conflict

I think this is a really useful self-reflection exercise in terms of identifying where your skills lie and where your deficits are. What is it that you need to develop in order to be more effective in a conflict situation? What you need to do is look at the list of statements and assess the extent to which you think you possess each of the following barriers to managing conflict effectively. These are as follows:

1. Poor follow up skills, i.e. you may continue to bear resentment even though you've agreed to a solution.

2. Poor contracting skills – your agreements may be stated insufficiently clearly and therefore not understood by either or both of you.

3. Poor anger management skills.

4. Poor problem solving skills.

5. Playing the defining game – this is something that stems from a competitive and combative attitude so when in conflict you may try to define yourself positively and the other party negatively.

6. Lack of openness.

7. Threatening vocal communication.

8. Threatening bodily communication.

9. Poor use of language.

10. Poor listening skills.

11. Bad timing.

12. Poor confrontation skills, i.e. you avoid acknowledging and owning your differences with another person or you have an inability to raise any issues at all.

13. Poor orientation to conflict – that is if you possess a realistic orientation you acknowledge that they are a part of life. You don't see them necessarily as a problem but you feel that they can be handled constructively.

14. A combative rather than collaborative attitude – you don't really want to have a win/win solution, you'd rather have a win/lose one and this is not appropriate.

What I'd like you to do here is to list, in rank order, the managing conflict barriers which you most feel need to change and then to feedback these to the group as a whole. It would be very interesting to see the similarities and differences between the areas that we feel we all need to develop in order to increase our skills in this area.

Activity 3

Role Play

This is a paired activity so I'd like you to pair up, perhaps with someone that you haven't worked with before. Within the context of this partnership I'd like you to think of either a current or a recent conflict that you have experienced in your life. Then Partner A can set the scene for the role play by describing the conflict and how each party behaves in it. Both parties then role play the conflict with Partner A trying to act as close as possible to how he or she would behave in conflicts.

We are going to video the role plays and then we are going to play these back with both partners having the opportunity to discuss which behaviours were helpful and which were harmful in managing this conflict. As a result of this, I would hope that Partner A would then be able to set himself or herself specific goals related perhaps to a previous activity as to how he/she can act or behave more effectively in this or other conflicts in the future. I'd then like you to reverse roles and repeat the cycle working on Partner B's conflict situation. I think that although role play is tricky for some of us (and it does take a lot of confidence initially to have a go at acting in this way), it's incredibly important in order to increase your awareness of your skills and particularly the current resources and deficits that you have. I'd also like to suggest that the more that we become an empathic, supportive, emotionally literate group of people, then it is less likely that individuals will experience feelings of stress around role play situations.

Activity 4

CUDSA – a five-stepped framework for managing conflict

This framework is taken from Richard Nelson-Jones' excellent book entitled, 'Human Relationship Skills' which is a training and self-help manual for developing these skills. It is a systematic approach to managing conflicts and I think that both in terms of personal relationships and professional relationships, it provides an extremely useful framework. The five steps are as follows:

1. **C**onfront the conflict.
2. **U**nderstand each other's position.
3. **D**efine the problem/problems.
4. **S**earch for and evaluate alternative solutions.
5. **A**gree upon and implement the best solutions.

This provides an easily understandable and memorable framework for all of us to use in managing conflicts. It is useful in that it provides a structure which we can really have a go at using even when the conflicts become very, very heated. This framework espouses the collaborative approach to managing conflicts which is exactly what we should be aspiring to within an emotionally literate context.

It encourages both individuals to make the sorts of choices that increase the chances of the course of the conflict being constructive as opposed to being destructive. It also avoids escalating the problem and really challenges each individual to co-operate in order to reduce resentment and feelings of violation. The idea overall is to gain the best possible outcome for all involved.

I'd now like us in Activity 4 to take ourselves through each step of this framework engaging in an activity at each stage of the process. There are, therefore, five sub-activities to Activity 4.

Exercise 4A – Step 1 – Confront the Conflict

What I'd like you to do in pairs is to think of one or two situations in your previous or current relationships where you have either tacitly or openly engaged in a conflict with someone. For each of the conflicts write out:

a) Your goals

b) A collusive, a combative and a collaborative way of confronting or failing to confront the other person with your view that there is a problem between you that needs solving. What I want you to remember here is that these terms: collusive, combative and collaborative, have been substituted for inhibited, aggressive and assertive.

c) If necessary, a request for time and space to work on the conflict.

I'd like you both to write out your responses to these questions and then discuss them. Alternatively, each of you could identify a conflict where it would be beneficial to use good skills in confronting the other person and to help each other decide on appropriate goals in managing these conflicts. You could then role play a collusive, combative and collaborative way of confronting or failing to confront the other person with a problem. It would then be helpful to feedback to the group as a whole, identifying any difficulties or positives as regards this process.

Exercise 4B – Step 2 – Understand each other's position

In order participate in this second step of the five-step framework, I'd like you to work in pairs with both of you again identifying a conflict that's personal to you. Partner A will then use his/her helpful responding skills to get Partner B to say in relation to this conflict (a) how he/she feels, (b) what he/she thinks, (c) how the other person feels, (d) what the other person thinks and (e) how the other person perceives Partner B's feelings and thoughts. Partner A will then listen as Partner B describes the other person's position in the first person, e.g. I am Tina. I don't like the way Billy treats me. My feelings are…….. My thoughts are…….. I think Billy's feelings are……… I think Billy's thoughts are ……… etc. It should then be possible for you to reverse roles prior to feeding back on these activities to the group as a whole.

Exercise 4C – Step 3 – Define the problems

In this activity what is important is to focus on collaborating to define problems accurately. There can be hidden agendas, unmet needs, the inability or ability to identify common ground and co-operating rather than competing to define problems as accurately and specifically as possible. What I'd like you to do is to work in pairs with Partner A using his/her helpful responding skills once again to enable Partner B to answer the following questions as regards to a conflict that they've recently or are currently experiencing (a) whether there are any hidden agendas and, if so, what they think they are, (b) what needs of each person need to be met or require meeting, (c) what common ground currently exists in this area of conflict, (d) provide as specific a definition as possible of the remaining problem or problems, (e) give your perception of your own contribution, if any, in sustaining this particular problem or difficulty. One each partner has been able to do this, i.e. answer the questions, they can then role play in regard to each of their conflicts (a) confronting the problem, (b) understanding each other's position, (c) defining the problems as specifically as possible in a genuine spirit of collaboration.

Exercise 4D – Step 4 – Search for and evaluate alternative solutions

In this activity I'd like you to work on your own and to once again consider a specific problem in one of your relationships and then write out:

1. As many possible solutions to this particular problem that you can think of in a 10 minute period without actually evaluating the merits of each solution.
2. Write out an evaluation of the advantages and disadvantages of your two most appealing solutions or the ones that you think would get you the best possible outcome.
3. Whether the solutions that you actually prefer are based on a combative 'I' when you lose or a collaborative 'I' when you win two approaches to the problems.

It would then be useful for all of us to feedback to the group as a whole. What is important here is that each of us is able to define our problems more specifically and accurately. It may be helpful, if some of us find this difficult, for us to join together as a group and thought storm in order to generate solutions for each other.

Exercise 4E – Step 5 – Agree upon and implement the best solutions

This activity is designed to help develop our skills in contracting or making agreements. The more that each of us owns an agreement, the less likely it is to be broken – that's basic common sense. But making agreements does involve clear and unambiguous communication and that's what we need to keep thinking about when we are actually engaging in this activity.

In this particular exercise I'd once again like you to do in pairs. Partner A and Partner B need to each have a conflict whose problems they've both defined and also to which they have searched for and evaluated alternative solutions.

I'd like to take the problem or problems in Partner A's conflict first in order to then discuss and agree upon the most acceptable solutions, to develop a plan for implementing the proposed solutions and then to discuss how they are going to evaluate how well the solutions actually turned out. Finally, they can discuss how they're going to handle any breaches of their agreement in the future. So there is a four-stepped process for each partner to move through. It would then be very helpful if we could ask each pair to feedback to the group as a whole.

Activity 5

Putting it all together

The idea here is to now put all the five steps of the CUDSA approach together. It would be helpful just to perhaps summarise once again what these are.

Step 1 - **C** - confronting the conflict
Step 2 - **U** - understanding each other's position
Step 3 - **D** - defining the problem or problems
Step 4 - **S** - search for and evaluating alternative solutions
Step 5 - **A** - agreeing upon and implementing your solution or solutions

What I'd like you to do here is to get into threes, perhaps with one of you acting as the observer for a role play exercise in which you work through each of these five steps, working on a current conflict that is worrying you. If a current conflict is unavailable, then it may be helpful to just think of something as recent as you possibly can. I'd like each of you to work out as specifically as possible how you would handle each of the sub-skills of the CUDSA process in managing this conflict effectively. In your threes, with one of you acting as observer, it would then be helpful to make use of your helpful responding skills in order to work through each of your conflicts, reversing roles and then feeding back to the group as a whole. I'd like us to really have some time then to discuss the implementation of this approach to managing conflict and how useful you feel it may be in both the school and home contexts.

I hope that this module has been helpful and that people genuinely do feel that this framework that we have discussed and used today may be useful to them in the future. What is important, is to really begin to recognise, both in ourselves and in each other, the range of skills and strategies that we have developed that we have and that we are effectively using in order to manage difficult situations in both the home and school context. It is vital that none of us just simply give up without actually really making the effort to use our relationship skills and the emotional literacy that we are continually developing in order to manage conflicts more effectively. Ultimately we are the ones who are responsible for how we behave. We have internal control and should be accountable for our behaviours and the way that we respond to others and to a variety of situations. It is that element of personal responsibility and accountability both to ourselves and to each other that needs to be reinforced here. If we are to create within the school context a truly empathic and supportive ethos, then each of us needs to take responsibility for our behaviours and for our own levels of emotional literacy and our self-management within both the social and classroom contexts.

Managing Conflicts

True or False?   Tick or cross against each Statement

1. Being able to search for mutually acceptable solutions is useful in handling conflicts.

2. Conflicts can result from misunderstanding rather than from genuine differences of interest.

3. Stresses that people experience in their own personal lives can make them prone to engage in destructive conflicts in their relationships.

4. If a conflict continues even though you've really tried to resolve it, you should really feel guilty about it.

5. In order to effectively manage conflict you need to have a very good repertoire of relevant skills.

6. Sometimes the strength of someone's emotions may narrow the scope of their vision within a conflict situation.

7. No-one holds a monopoly on the truth.

8. Tit-for-tat is generally considered fair play.

9. Being able to manage conflicts in a relationship is best viewed as an exercise in joint problem solving for mutual benefit.

10. A conflict can never have a positive outcome.

11. More often than not, people who try to handle conflicts cooperative are likely to be taken advantage of.

12. In order to win a conflict you need to always compete as hard as possible.

13. Sometimes people can be ruled by their fears when in conflict.

14. In order to manage differences we need to have a clear picture of what these differences actually are.

15. It is often better to avoid differences than face up to them within a relationship.

16. Effective management of conflicts needs people to be able to discipline their thinking appropriately.

17. It pays to act on impulse in a conflict situation.

18. People who tend to carry around a great deal of unfinished business and pain from their relationships with their parents are less inclined to engage in destructive conflicts than those who do not.

19. Conflicts are perhaps best approached in a climate of mutual respect and tolerance.

20. Intimate partners can be capable of changing both themselves and the quality of their relationships.

21. Those who feel that others must be perfect sexual partners place unrealistic expectations on them.

22. Men and women are both psychologically and physically different.

23. People who truly care about their partners and know one another should always be able to sense each other's needs and preferences without having to be told them.

24. Listening appropriately and understanding the other's viewpoint is a useful skill in managing a conflict.

25. People tend to be rational in conflict situations.

26. It's never helpful to express anger when in conflict with another.

27. Don't ever admit to your contribution to sustaining a conflict.

28. It is often helpful to blame the other person in a conflict.

29. A useful way of managing a conflict is to talk about it with third parties rather than with the person directly involved.

30. The less aggressive people are during conflicts, the more likely they are to achieve a desirable outcome.

Module 5

> ### Your Skills and Deficits in Managing Conflict

Look at the list of statements and assess the extent to which you think you possess each of the following barriers to managing conflict effectively. These are as follows:

1. Poor follow up skills, i.e. you may continue to bear resentment even though you've agreed to a solution.

2. Poor contracting skills – your agreements may be stated insufficiently clearly and therefore not understood by either or both of you.

3. Poor anger management skills.

4. Poor problem solving skills.

5. Playing the defining game – this is something that stems from a competitive and combative attitude so when in conflict you may try to define yourself positively and the other party negatively.

6. Lack of openness.

7. Threatening vocal communication.

8. Threatening bodily communication.

9. Poor use of language.

10. Poor listening skills.

11. Bad timing.

12. Poor confrontation skills, i.e. you avoid acknowledging and owning your differences with another person or you have an inability to raise any issues at all.

13. Poor orientation to conflict – that is if you possess a realistic orientation you acknowledge that they are a part of life. You don't see them necessarily as a problem but you feel that they can be handled constructively.

14. A combative rather than collaborative attitude – you don't really want to have a win/win solution, you'd rather have a win/lose one and this is not appropriate.

Emotionally Literate Behaviour Management

MODULE 6

Putting it all together - Coaching

EMOTIONALLY LITERATE BEHAVIOUR MANAGEMENT

MODULE 6 – PUTTING IT ALL TOGETHER - COACHING

Introduction

At the start of this module it is important initially just to focus on reassessing your own relationship skills; the kind of skills that we all need in order to maintain and develop good relationships within both our staff teams and personal relationships and in relationships with the students that we teach. I want us to think about how we can further develop and maintain those skills in order to then make use of them within the process of coaching.

What I'm talking about here is a solution-focused tool for peer support within the school context. Now that we've covered the skills of emotional literacy in terms of being able to identify and label our feelings, being good and effective listeners, being able to define and assert ourselves and manage our stress and angry emotions and feelings and being able to manage conflict effectively, we can pool all those skills together in order utilise them within a solution focused coaching framework. This is probably the best form of peer support for teachers that I have found in the last couple of years and I'd consequently say that if we are going to have emotionally literate teachers within an emotionally literate context, then this is the approach that they should be adopting. This is essential if they are to maintain themselves as effective teachers who manage themselves and the behaviour within themselves and their classrooms most effectively.

Activity 1

Assessing your relationship skills and deficits

What I'd like you to do in pairs is to look at the check list that you're going to receive now and focus on each of the key skills, considering which ones you feel that you've managed to develop further and which you would identify as specific deficits on which you need to continue to work. Then discuss these with a partner and perhaps feed back to the group as a whole at the end of the activity so that we can identify any similarities and differences and consider the kinds of resources we might need as a group in order to move on further. The skills are as follows:

1. Having an attitude of personal responsibility for how you relate and behave.
2. Having a good knowledge of concepts and terms with which to understand how you and others relate to each other.
3. Being able to express your feelings and being in touch with them at all times.
4. Being able to start a positive relationship.

5. Being able to develop relationships through the ways in which you talk about yourself.

6. Being able to listen with real accuracy to others and understand them.

7. Responding helpfully to other people so that they can talk to you and, if necessary, further clarify their own problems and concerns.

8. Being able to manage your feelings of anger and stress.

9. Being able to effectively manage conflict so as to enable positive solutions and outcomes.

Activity 2

Maintaining your skills

In this exercise I'd like each of you to consider as many of the pressures that you can possibly think of in each of the following categories that might hinder you from maintaining and further developing your skills. Consider the following areas:

1. Pressures from within yourself.
2. Pressures from others.
3. Pressures from your broader environment.

Next try and identify those that you consider to be potentially the most harmful to you and also then consider the kinds of strategies that you are going to need to develop in order to combat these harmful pressures. When we've all done that it would be very interesting to allow some time to feed back and to discuss our strategies as I'm sure that this would enable all of us to see a way forward.

Introducing Coaching

So, what is teacher coaching? I would suggest that it's an emotionally literate tool for supporting and developing teachers' classroom management skills. We can do this in a safe, supportive way where teachers feel that their own personal concerns and needs are addressed by colleagues who are non-judgemental and skilled in listening and providing emotional support to others. Teachers who are emotionally literate are best able and better able to support their colleagues and this method of peer support – the coaching role – is probably one of the best methods of providing each other with tools to support the process of change and provide really useful, meaningful and practical advice.

We know in schools what really concerns us and that is the behaviour of the children. It's their emotional responses to us and their behavioural responses to us and the way in which we deal with them that perhaps most impacts on their learning and our ability to maintain our own mental health and to manage the classroom effectively. The central aim of this series has, to date, been for us to look at our own behaviour and how that impacts on the students and others around us and how we can best develop our own skills.

It is now time to also begin to consider, once we have developed these skills, how we can maintain that development and how that will impact positively upon the way in which we manage our classrooms.

So, how can we do this? I think that one of the tools that may well provide an answer for us is teacher coaching. The idea is that we as individuals, emotionally literate teachers, professional colleagues, can actually help each other develop the skills that we need to be able to manage. We can act as enablers and we can help and ensure the professional development of our peers.

Coaching is essentially a process of observation and feedback. The rationale for this process is that as individuals we don't always recognise the specific nature of what we do that is actually effective. Very often in the classroom situation we can be doing something that is really good and working but we don't realise it ourselves. It is only when someone else comes in, observes it and highlights it for us and also helps us to generalise those skills that we already have that we become more self-aware.

The balance of support and challenge within this coaching process is clearly crucial in terms of increasing the likelihood of positive change. The use of joint problem solving, is also a very powerful tool for promoting rather than imposing change. Coaching is also not just about professional development and professional skills. It is also about our personal development. It is about us as people. That's why I think it is an emotionally literate tool and that's why the skills that we've been developing and we've been focusing on are so essential here. I think it was Taylor that said, 'Personal and professional development are one and the same thing'. I would hope that this process of coaching which takes us from the beginning, a starting point to an end point, can help us to really develop both ourselves and our skills and strategies as professional teachers.

What I want to highlight here, particularly in terms of classroom behaviour management, is the 'just do it like this' syndrome. This is not what this is about. Teacher coaching is about making use of a range of solution focused techniques which can help us to support each other in the most positive way and find solutions and move ourselves forward. Within that there is continually a focus upon what is actually working, what we are doing well and on reinforcing and further developing the self-esteem and emotional wellbeing of all the teachers in the school context.

So what does coaching involve? Basically it involves two teachers acting within a mutual support system who observe and then provide feedback. They observe each other in the classroom context and then provide feedback in a very structured way, making use of solution focused techniques. I'm going to be providing you with formats for teacher coaching which can be used subsequent to the delivery of this session. Once you have observed someone for, say, a lesson (a 45 minute period) you then need have an equal amount of time to sit down together and for the person who has been observing to actually talk to the teacher and feed back on what they've seen, what they've heard, and to also highlight the skills and strategies that they have seen that teacher displaying so that they can then be built upon. It's an observe and feedback situation and within that feedback the following techniques are generally used.

The first one is 'problem free talk'. This is a period of time when you talk purely about what has gone well - that's a very good opening for this interview i.e. not focusing on any problems at all. Then we can use the notion of exception finding. For example, if we do find that perhaps one student in the classroom has been having some difficulties or there is a problem, we ask the question, when does this not occur, when is this not the case? If there is a 'stuck situation' or the teacher wishes to move on in a significant way, we may ask the miracle question. For example, what would this classroom be like if you woke up tomorrow and a miracle had happened overnight, someone waved a magic wand over you and the whole situation? You woke up, you walked into the classroom and it was absolutely brilliant, fantastic. It was a miracle lesson, miracle class. How would that be different to what's currently happening? And then, of course, in order to get to that kind of miracle state, the next technique that you might use would be rating scales. For example, on a scale of 1-10 where do you think you are now in terms of managing this class effectively? Where would you like to be on a scale of 1-10 if you could move forward? And then goal setting. What do we need to do? What do you need to do? And what needs to happen in order to support you further in terms of getting too that higher number on the rating scale and to achieve your goals?

So, Teacher Coaching is a solution focused interview technique and a set of skills that we are going to now practice together.

Activity 3

Problem-free talk

Problem-free talk is basically what begins the feedback process. This is a time when the two individuals can discuss what has been observed and their feelings about the situation but in an extremely positive manner, no focusing on any negatives whatsoever. This isn't easy for many of us because if we actually reflect upon the extent to which we use negative language or make disparaging comments about ourselves or others on a daily basis, I would imagine that for the majority of us we do far more of this negative talk than making positive comments. Why is this? I think it's really important to have a go at this; to sit down and actually engage in what I call 'problem-free talk'. So the activity here that I'd like you to undertake is to spend the next 10 minutes discussing things that you feel really good and positive about in your lives, sharing them with a partner and attempting not to make any negative or disparaging comment about yourself or another person or situation.

Activity 4

Exception Finding

Exception finding is really a way of finding out when things are 'different' i.e. so when doesn't this happen? When is that child actually focused on task, not bothering you, not shouting out, not being aggressive to others – what's happening then, what's different about that context? And even if the behaviour is very, very slightly better, what is it that is actually making that slight exception, that slight improvement, that slight difference? This kind of exception finding allows us to identify opportunities for looking at and focusing on strengths and coping strategies as opposed to the negatives. It also allows the teacher to bring their own skills, their own strengths to a situation that they may have found very difficult previously and felt quite 'stuck in'. So it is a way of getting out of the 'stuckness' of a situation. The move forward might be extremely small initially but it can then lead on, I think, to greater change.

In your pairs I'd like each of you to identify one situation within your own current classrooms that you have some concerns about. This may be an individual or a group of individuals with whom you are finding relationships difficult. You may be finding some difficulties in maintaining them on task or maintaining positive behaviours. Once you've done this, I'd then like you to think of a time when the situation has been better, however, slight. Why was it better? What was making or contributing to this being a better situation? What was happening? What things were happening that you would like to see continue? What's different about the times when it goes better and what other things are happening at these times that you would like to see continue? Focus on those questions, taking it in turns to ask them of each other and then feedback to the group as a whole.

Activity 5

Preferred futures, ratings and setting goals

As you continue your interviews in pairs, I'd like you not to focus more specifically on a school or classroom situation. I'd like you to bring this back to your own personal lives and to identify something that you would like to change; possibly within yourself, within a relationship at home or your social context. Consider this situation and ask each other the following questions:

The first one is the miracle question. I'd like you to image that you go to bed tonight and whilst you are asleep someone waves a magic wand over you and when you wake up things have changed and they really have changed for the better. Everything's okay. You're feeling good. The situation is fine. How would you feel when your hopes are realised and your problem seems to have disappeared? What would this look like and how would it feel to you? Try to describe this picture of your preferred future in as much detail as possible. Then I'd like you to have a go at using a rating scale. Ask your partner on a scale of 0-10 with 0 being the worst that things have been in your life and 10 representing how you want things to be; where would you put yourself now at this point in time. Then say what is it that means you're at this level or number and not at 0. For example, if you are on 3 or 4 tell me what you're doing or what you have done in order to get to that level and not to be at zero.

Next, I'd like you to ask each other what you need to do in order to get to the next point on the scale or to get to the point on the scale where you feel you would be nearer to your miracle situation. What would be happening and how would you feel if you were higher on this scale or as high as you wanted to be? The final part of this interview is to then set goals, asking your partner what they need to do, in order to move further up this rating scale. Once you've both had a go at using this series of questions and engaging in identifying the preferred future using the rating scales, I'd like you to consider how this can all be drawn together within the teacher coaching approach by referring to the classroom observation schedule provided in the next activity.

Activity 6

Teacher Coaching

This is, in effect, what I would call a 'take home' task. What I'd like you to do, in order to reinforce the concepts that we have covered today, is to make use of the teacher coaching classroom observation schedule provided and to arrange in pairs to observe each other within the classroom context, in the next few weeks. Make use of this observation check list and then feed back via the consultation process in which you can make use of the solution-focused strategies and techniques practised today. The classroom observation schedule is fairly straightforward, identifying the teacher, the date, the class size, boys/girls, absentees, key players, support that's available and perhaps a seating plan and then encourages you to consider under a range of headings as to the nature and management of that particular lesson. I think that this is quite a helpful framework on which to pin your observations. Most important, of course, is to remember always to focus on the fact that you are emotionally literate teachers working within an emotionally literate context which means that the end result should be something empathic, supportive and entirely positive. The idea here is that you should feel nurtured and looked after so that, in turn, you can successfully and effectively nurture, look after and manage the students that you teach on a daily basis.

Activity 7

Plenary and contracts

In the last part of this session I think we should engage in briefly reviewing what we've covered in the Modules to date and ask ourselves what we think we've learnt. How valuable or otherwise do we feel the course as a whole and the skills covered have been to us as individuals and as a group?

Finally, the second part of this activity is for us all to sign up to contracts which will, hopefully, help to ensure that we continue to develop as emotionally literate professionals who work within the kind of empathic context which fosters and promotes positive change in relationships and mental and physical wellbeing. I have provided a dummy contract, i.e. one that you may wish to sign up to. However, it may be more appropriate for each of you to devise your own contracts in which you include the kinds of commitments that you feel are truly pertinent to yourself as individuals. The contract I've provided is as follows:

1. As an individual person I am ultimately responsible for my feelings, thoughts and behaviours within all of my relationships.
2. I commit myself to using, maintaining and further developing my skills of emotional literacy within all my relationships.
3. I also commit myself to help others whom I work with and relate to, to use and maintain and develop their own emotional literacy skills.
4. The skills that I commit myself to using, maintaining and developing, include keeping in touch with my feelings; beginning and maintaining appropriate relationships; being prepared to further develop relationships by being open and honest at all times; listening to and helping others to feel really understood; responding in a helpful way to other people in the school context and in the social context; effectively and constructively managing my feelings of stress and anger; managing conflict constructively; maintaining and further developing my ability to effectively coach others within a solution-focused framework.

I know that I will make mistakes and fall short of my goals on some occasions. However, I commit myself to persisting in attempting to honour this contract.

Signed: Date:

The contract should be posted or pinned to a board in an obvious place as a reminder to you.

Module 6 Activity 1

Assessing your relationship skills and deficits

Do you have these skills? What do you need to develop? What resources might help you? DISCUSS!

Key Skills

1. Having an attitude of personal responsibility for how you relate and behave.

2. Having a good knowledge of concepts and terms with which to understand how you and others relate to each other.

3. Being able to express your feelings and being in touch with them at all times.

4. Being able to start a positive relationship.

5. Being able to develop relationships though the ways in which you talk about yourself.

6. Being able to listen with real accuracy to others and understand them.

7. Responding helpfully to other people so that they can talk to you and, if necessary, further clarify their own problems and concerns.

8. Being able to manage your feelings of anger and stress.

9. Being able to effectively manage conflict so as to enable positive solutions and outcomes.

Module 6 – Activity 7

A Personal Contract

1. As an individual person I am ultimately responsible for my feelings, thoughts and behaviours within all of my relationships.

2. I commit myself to using, maintaining and further developing my skills of emotional literacy within all my relationships.

3. I also commit myself to help others whom I work with and relate to, to use and maintain and develop their own emotional literacy skills.

4. The skills that I commit myself to using, maintaining and developing, include keeping in touch with my feelings; beginning and maintaining appropriate relationships; being prepared to further develop relationships by being open and honest at all times; listening to and helping others to feel really understood; responding in a helpful way to other people in the school context and in the social context; effectively and constructively managing my feelings of stress and anger; managing conflict constructively; maintaining and further developing my ability to effectively coach others within a solution-focused framework.

Signed _____

Date _____

Module 6

<table>
<tr><td colspan="2" align="center">Teacher Coaching
A Classroom Observation Schedule</td></tr>
<tr><td>Teacher</td><td></td></tr>
<tr><td>Date</td><td></td></tr>
<tr><td>Class size – Boys
         Girls
         Absentees
         Key Players</td><td></td></tr>
<tr><td>Support staff available</td><td></td></tr>
<tr><td>Seating Plan</td><td></td></tr>
<tr><td></td><td></td></tr>
<tr><td></td><td></td></tr>
<tr><td></td><td></td></tr>
</table>

Introduction to the lesson

Relationships

Esteem/safety

Routines/organisation

Management style (e.g. Patience, low-key, certainly not severity, pre-emptive, layering)

Teaching and Learning

Gaining class attention

Voice

Expectations
Re- Work

Behaviour

Praise (systems and use)

Development areas

Emotionally Literate Behaviour Management

MODULE 7

10 Most Useful Strategies

EMOTIONALLY LITERATE BEHAVIOUR MANAGEMENT

MODULE 7 – 10 MOST USEFUL STRATEGIES OR TOP TIPS

Introduction

In this module we will now begin to focus specifically upon our own teaching styles and attitudes and the way in which all schooling issues and contexts can impact upon these areas. We will also have the opportunity to consider our classroom practice and to specifically reflect upon the way in which we currently manage behaviour within the classroom context. We will naturally, continually be required to reflect upon our own parts in each interaction and whether or not we were responding and acting in an emotionally literate way so as to ensure the best possible outcome for all involved.

There will also be an opportunity to consider ten tried and tested 'most useful strategies'. These will be introduced by a series of video clips in which teachers can reflect upon specific scenarios. These will be typical of the kinds of difficulties that teachers face in mainstream classrooms on a daily basis. There will be an opportunity to consider what went wrong for the teacher involved and why this situation may have deteriorated. Teachers would also have the opportunity to discuss what those involved may have done differently in order to achieve a better outcome for themselves, how could they have reacted? What would have been the most appropriate response? What kinds of skills and strategies would have been most appropriate to use? There could also be opportunity for teachers to consider what they may have done themselves in this same situation and to discuss and share their own strategies, skills and knowledge base at this point.

Activity 1

Looking at Your Own Style and Attitudes

In this activity I would like you to carefully read through the questionnaire. Here you have six points to divide between the three options for each question. The more that you agree with a particular statement the more the six points you should award to it. For example, you may feel that 1a is worth five points whilst 1b is worth one point and 1c is worth 0 points. You need to use all six points for each question and to enter these in the boxes on the right-hand side of the page. What is vital here is that you are honest about your views, feelings and thoughts. Your responses need to be authentic otherwise there is no real point in continuing with such an activity. It is important to remember that the idea here is to begin to challenge yourself to think about why you hold the kinds of attitudes and ideas that you do and whether or not these are gaining you the best possible outcomes in the classroom context. It is also an opportunity to discuss your ideas with peers and colleagues and to further develop your skills and approaches in the light of their feedback. An additional payback on this activity is the further development of the sense of peer support within what is now, hopefully, an emotionally literate framework and context.

Activity 2

Whole School Issues

In this exercise I would like you to work in pairs in order to complete the questionnaire provided. Once again, it is vital that the task is approached in an honest and transparent manner. If there are difficulties within the school context of things that need to be changed or further adjusted in order to enable you to be a more emotionally literate teacher, and more successful in managing behaviour of the students you teach then the results of this questionnaire should begin to prompt such a process of change. It should be possible to identify key areas for further development.

After answering the series of questions it should be possible to work together in order to identify key targets in the following areas:

- Peer support – how can this be further developed and how can we further create an emotionally literate atmosphere of support amongst colleagues.
- Whole school policies – how well is the Behaviour Policy currently working and can the effectiveness of this tool be further improved.
- Parental involvement – are we really making full and effective use of communications with our parents and carers.
- School culture and ethos – is the school ethos and core values clearly defined, explicit and emotionally literate. Are all the stakeholders involved and are these values communicated appropriately to them?
- External agency support – what can we do in terms of accessing this support and are we currently able to call upon such external agency support at an appropriate stage, i.e. to avoid exclusion as the only resort.

What is most important here is that you now discuss your findings and share your ideas so that we can begin to develop a way forward, identifying the kinds of changes that we need to make to the school context in order to further ensure that all of us feel that we are effective practitioners and empowered to continue to be so.

Activity 3

Classroom Practice

This is self-reflection activity and it is particularly important to consider each area in some depth. If we don't know what we are doing, how we are doing it and why we are doing it then we are not reflective practitioners and we will be unable to change the way in which we function within the school context. This questionnaire asks you to reflect upon the following key areas.

- Planning and preparation
- What you do before the lesson
- Lesson openings
- Your body language
- Relationships
- Questioning

- Giving instructions
- Maintaining discipline
- New methodology
- The room layout and design
- The use of praise and encouragements
- Your lesson endings.

There is also an opportunity for you to reflect upon possible points for action. This can be done through discussion with colleagues. It may well be the case that this will be an extremely useful opportunity to work collaboratively. How can we support each other in developing our classroom practice? What is it that your colleague does that you feel may be a useful strategy or resource to you? How can you ensure that these skills are shared and the information disseminated appropriately? Once again, I feel it is extremely important to emphasise the importance of this emotionally literate and supportive framework in context. In order to effectively develop our practice we need to feel supported and empowered. Perhaps it is now, once again, time for us to arrange a series of teacher/coaching sessions providing each other with mutual support through this process of observation and feedback.

Activity 4

Ten Most Useful Strategies

In this final element of module 7 you are going to be presented with a series of ten scenarios. Each of these reflects the ten top tips that I would recommend to anyone who has to walk into a mainstream classroom and effectively manage the emotions and behaviour of the students
included within that context. For each of these top tips you are going to see a short video clip. In each clip the teacher being observed reacts in a negative way and pays no attention to the advice on offer here. The idea here is for you to observe the behaviours yourselves and to then discuss what that teacher may have done differently in order to achieve a better outcome.

These teachers are not intended to be examples of perfect practitioners, but are clearly all trying their hardest to do a good job. It is important to think about what is getting in the way of some of them being able to effectively manage the behaviour of the students in their classrooms. There is a really good opportunity here for you to all discuss in smaller groups
what you might do differently and what the best response would be. What are the strategies and skills that you would need in each of these situations. How would you cope most effectively? How would you manage your feelings? How would you manage your behaviour and their feelings?

The ten top tips (with a scenario for each one) are as follow:

- keep your emotions under control
- don't challenge the student in a confrontational way, but challenge the behaviour
- students' behaviour is taught, learnt and contextual
- plan your lessons

- always try to be consistent
- try to involve the students in planning to improve their learning environment
- teach the way in which the students actually learn, i.e. look at their learning styles and preferences
- keep on developing your practice
- be unpredictable at times (only in your teaching style!)
- always share the burden with colleagues

I hope that this session has enabled you to further reflect upon your own practice and begin to formulate ideas regarding future changes that you might make in yourself, in your practice and in the cultural ethos of your learning context.

Module 7 – Emotionally Literate Behaviour Management

Looking at Your Own Styles and Attitudes

Classroom Management Styles – Key Characteristics

You have six points to divide between the three options for each question, the more you agree with a statement, the more of the six points you should award it. For example, you may feel 1a is worth 4 points, 1b 2 points and 1c 0 points – Use all 6 points for each question and enter them in the boxes on the right.

Example

Question 1 a) [4]

b) [2]

c) [0]

When completing the questionnaire, be honest with yourself in answering how you would normally respond to the situations described, NOT how you feel you should behave or think. In this way, you will obtain most benefit when putting the results to practical use in developing your skills and approach.

1. a) I basically like children and want children to like me. ☐

   b) In order to meet the needs of the majority I need to have some consensus from the children on the standards of their behaviour and attitudes. ☐

   c) I think children prefer t have a structured, orderly, calm and disciplined environment. ☐

2. Children …
   a) generally want to learn. ☐

   b) if left to their own devices, can tend to be naturally anarchic and bolshy ☐

   c) are individual and will best respond to a warm and empathic approach. ☐

3. As a teacher…
   a) I believe that I have a right to expect children to obey me and follow instructions straight away. ☐

   b) I believe that behaviour can be learned. ☐

   c) I believe that most children want their teachers' approval and respect. ☐

4. I have an ambition to …
   a) encourage individuality in children. ☐

   b) always get the very best from my children – both academically and socially. ☐

   c) let my children be themselves. ☐

5. I manage my classes best… .
   a) by giving generous praise and positive feedback ☐

   b) by well developed relationships, humour and stimulating and
   engaging teaching ☐

   c) through creating a quiet, orderly environment and through my own
   personality. ☐

6. When I am faced with unacceptable behaviour …
   a) my first approach is to defuse the situation and try to find out the underlying
   cause. ☐

   b) I will usually insist on following the steps outlined in the school's discipline
   policy. ☐

   c) my instinct is to defuse potential confrontations with a verbal reprimand
   which is easily understood. ☐

7. When a child refuses to follow an instruction …
   a) I will usually insist and point out the penalties if the disobedience continues. ☐

   b) I will usually not make an issue of the fact at the time but challenge the
   child later about their actions – generally in a 1:1 context. ☐

   c) I can usually either cajole the individual into the desired behaviour or
   tactically ignore the situation. ☐

8. a) Get the behaviour of children right at the outset and then good learning
   will follow. ☐

   b) Children's friendship groups are crucially important in the development
   of learning in the classroom. ☐

   d) Carefully arranging group dynamics will help assist in the learning process. ☐

9. Praise and encouragement …
   a) is a vital strategy for me and can't be over used. ☐

   b) is the corner stone of raising the self esteem in disaffected and less
   able pupils ☐

   c) can be patronising; I prefer to use it infrequently but give plenty of
   objective and constructive feedback. ☐

10. I believe that I should …
    a) be a positive role model, give children confidence and be consistent in my
    approach. ☐

    b) create a learning environment which isn't boring and defuse potential
    confrontations. ☐

    c) make individual pupils feel accountable for the outcomes of inappropriate
    behaviour. ☐

11. a) Telling someone precisely what is required and then how to go about it,
    then monitoring the results closely, is always the safest way of ensuring
    that the work is done to your specifications/requirements. ☐

    b) It is always important to respect children's dignity and self esteem by
    suggesting rather than telling them what to do. ☐

92

c) Being explicit and clear about what is required and the standards expected is usually helpful and the best way to maintain a happy classroom.

12. When things go wrong or mistakes are made I tend to...
a) try to use the situation as a problem solving and learning opportunity.

b) reassert direction and get things back on track, i.e. taking the lead.

c) smooth things over and reassure the students that it doesn't matter.

Now transfer these scores to the table below using the spaces available in each column.

For example, if Question 1 scores in   a) [4]   b) [2]   c) [0]

	Column 1			Column 2			Column 3		
	a	b	c	a	b	c	a	b	c
Question 1	▦	2	▦	4	▦	▦	▦	▦	0

Now total up all the figures in each column. Then have a look at the feedback on the next page and discuss with colleagues.

Total Column 1 [   ]   Total Column 2 [   ]   Total Column 3 [   ]

Module 7 Looking at your own Styles and Attitudes

Feedback from the Self Assessment

Whatever your views on this kind of self diagnosis tool, the survey may well demonstrate that you use all three styles at some time, moving between them to meet different circumstances. The survey may also show that you have a preferred style, one that you use more often or retreat to when under pressure.

COLUMN 1	COLUMN 2	COLUMN 3
Enabler	Imposer	Appealer

This assessment should help you to reflect upon your style(s) and consider the use of the other skills in appropriate circumstances. There is no right or wrong approach – each is valid in its place.

If you would like to take this further, it may be useful for you to ask a colleague to observe you or use a tape recorder to record your interactions with children using a similar table to the one below, ticking off your verbal characteristics every time they occur.

	Enabling		Imposing		Appealing
	What we agreed we could do		What I want you to do is…		What I would really like you to do, is….
	We agreed that your full attention is vital for demonstrations…		Pens down everyone, now, look this way.		Is there any chance you could all look this way please…
	We said you don't want to waste our time so start as quickly as you can..		Straight away. Don't waste time…		It would be really helpful if you could start now…
	Rather than waste time if you finish you can prepare for the next lesson be reading page 3…		I expect everyone to start the exercise in the next chapter when you finish the classwork…		If you finish your work you could turn to the next chapter and read the first page…
	(add further "enabling" examples)		(add further "imposing examples)		(add further "appealing" examples)

Module 7 – Whole School Issues

Would you seek advice from a colleague to help modify the behaviour of a challenging pupil?

☐	No. Because It would be seen as an admission of failure by my colleagues.
☐	No. Because the climate in the school does not lend itself to support.
☐	Sometimes. I have been able to identify those staff who are supportive.
☐	Always. Effective management has created a climate where, as a staff we.

are encouraged to support each other and share strategies for managing inappropriate pupil behaviour

To what extent do you feel that there is a supportive, collaborative ethos in your school?

	1	2	3	4	5	6	7	8	9	10	
(Low)											(High)

At what point should parents be involved in helping to manage pupil behaviour in school?

☐	Not at all.
☐	Immediately a problem arises in the classroom/school.
☐	When there have been a number of incidents of inappropriate behaviour.
☐	When a pupil is close to being excluded and a Pupil Support Programme is being developed.
☐	Other? Specify.

Think about your own school. What steps are taken to actively inform and involve parents in the process of helping pupils modify their behaviour?

	Often	Sometimes	Never
The main contact with parents is made when behavioural problems arise.			
Parents are informed of pupils' **positive** achievements on a regular basis.			
Support is provided for parents in working with their children. Parents are actively encouraged to visit and support the school.			

Points for consideration

Module 7 – Whole School Issues contd..

- **Peer Support**
  What needs to be in place and how could the present system of peer support be developed. How can I create an atmosphere of support amongst my colleagues?

- **Whole School Policies**
  How well are your whole school behaviour policies working for you and how could their effectiveness be improved:

- **Parents**
  Are you making full and effective use of communications with parents?

- **School Ethos and Culture**
  Does your school have a clearly defined ethos and core values? Are these communicated to all stakeholders?

External Support
Do you call upon external support agencies for support at an early enough stage so exclusion is not the only resort>

Points for consideration

Module 7 – Practice in the Classroom

Planning and preparation

Does the lesson planning concentrate on content and neglect how to teach it?
What factors affect your preparation for a lesson (change of room/building, non specialist classroom, lack of suitable resources, lack of quality time)?
What can be done to help in this process?
Does your planning recognise different learning styles?
Actions

Before the lesson

What are your views about children entering a classroom formally or informally?

- [ ] I can see no need to change the current practice.
- [ ] It is not possible to ask children to line up in a corridor because of the physical problems this might bring or that other classes don't line up.
- [ ] I intend to adopt a change of approach for pupils entering a classroom.

Other

If you are not physically able to be at a classroom to meet a class then can colleagues in neighbouring classrooms help?
Do you know which lesson a problematic group has had before your lesson?
Do you use a seating plan to isolate difficult individuals or not allow unco-operative pupils to congregate at the margins of the room?
Actions

Lesson openings

Do you consider there are changes that you can adopt to improve the start of your lesson? – Do you greet the class, put them at their ease?

Do your instructions both set the learning objectives and recall what they have previously learnt and then keep reinforcing them throughout the lesson?

Do your lessons open on a positive note, setting high expectations and praise for the past achievements, capturing interest and stimulating enthusiasm?

Do you have a strategy for dealing with the vexed issue of latecomers and minimising the disruptive influence they may have?

Are your openings too long?

Actions

Body language

Does your body language send out positive messages, especially at the start and end of lessons?

Consider the way in which you greet children at the start of the morning or afternoon sessions as well as those who arrive at your classroom for each lesson.

Actions

Relationships

Separating the behaviour from the person is key, but sometimes difficult to achieve. How can we demonstrate that we value everyone?

Background knowledge is vital; do your systems facilitate the communication of good information and data about children?

Do you take informal opportunities to find out small things about children, their goals or aspirations, likes and dislikes?

The use of humour, trust and interaction are techniques that work to build relationships; are there everyday opportunities you can use?

Actions

Questioning

Are you sensitive to the style and type of questioning, ensuring that you create an atmosphere of trust and respect in your classroom?

Do you pay enough attention to ensuring that older pupils are challenged and that both boys and girls are encouraged to think and answer?

Do you use a wide range of questioning styles, including open and closed?

How do the questions help learning?

Actions

Giving instructions

Have you considered the number of instructions in a statement?

Do you find that instructions have to be repeated several times before they are acted upon?

Are you a shouter? Do you use your voice well to arouse and sustain interest or signal key points in the lesson? Are you quiet? A detached, unmodulated or continually strident tone invites pupils to "switch off".

Have you ever used signals instead of verbal instructions?

Module 7 – Practice in the Classroom contd…

Maintaining discipline

Are you clear and consistent in implementing the school's discipline guidelines?

Are you fair and explicit in the way you interpret and implement the basic procedures in effectively managing classes?

Do your pupils know the guidelines or are they frequently reminded of the accepted standards of behaviour? Do they agree with them and feel they are fair?

Do you use the school reward system consistently and ensure that all age groups received credit and appropriate praise?

Actions

Methodology

Do you control entry and seating, give clear instructions and explanations?

How much "middle" is there to the lesson? A lesson might have several openings.

Do you regularly use interesting materials and stimulating activities?

Do you challenge and support your pupils, set high expectations, keep on task and respond fully to their work?

Are weaknesses in basic skills addressed sympathetically and pupils taught to work independently and efficiently?

Do you employ techniques for maintaining concentration and enthusiasm for commitment?

Have you considered the various learning styles in your classes?

Actions

Room design and layout

Does your classroom facilitate effective learning and support good class management?

Are there any alterations that may help? Is you your classroom bright, tidy and welcoming?

What do your children feel about the classroom? Do you know?

Actions

Module 7 – Practice in the Classroom contd...

Praise and encouragement
Indicate which pair of statement you agree and which you disagree with.

	Agree	Disagree
Praise is a reward given for completed achievement. Encouragement is an acknowledgment of effort.		
Praise tells students they've satisfied the demands of others. Encouragement helps students evaluate their own performance.		
Praise connects students' work with their personal worth. Encouragement focuses on strength of the work, helping students see and feel confident in their own ability.		
Praise can place a "cold judgement" on the student as person Encouragement show acceptance and respect.		
Praise can be withheld as punishment or cheapened by overuse. Encouragement can be freely given because everyone deserves to receive it.		
Praise can be patronising when it's "talking down". The praise can enjoy a superior position. Encouragement is a message between equals.		

Actions

Lesson endings

How can the lesson ending be improved? Do you plan your end of lesson phases with a resume of the learning points, a summary of the objectives achieved?
Do you have a clock in the room to assist you in timing and pacing the lesson?
Do you build anticipation for the next lesson?
Do students review their own learning?
How is the plenary managed?
Is dismissal a positive and courteous event?
Actions

Module 7 – Emotionally Literate Behaviour Management – Scenario Reflection Format

- What was the situation?

- What went wrong for the student(s) and why?

- What went wrong for the teacher and why?

- What do you think the teacher could have done differently in order to handle the situation more effectively? (include specific strategies).

- How would you have reacted and how useful do you think your reactions would have been in the situation?

- What do you think would achieve the best outcome for **all** involved?

Emotionally Literate Behaviour Management

MODULE 8

Action Planning and Review

EMOTIONALLY LITERATE BEHAVIOUR MANAGEMENT

MODULE 8 – ACTION PLANNING AND REVIEW

Introduction

In this session you will have an opportunity to review the contents of the course to date and to also formulate your own personal action plans for the future. This is probably best done via a less formal discussion in which everyone participating can air their views, identifying things that they feel have been key aspects or important aspects of the course whilst also focusing on possibilities for the future and identifying specific changes that may need to be made both as individuals and as a group.

Activity 1

In order to review the topics covered and identify key learning areas it would be helpful to thought storm a very simple question. What have we learnt about emotionally literate behaviour management? This thought storm may include:

- the key skills of emotional literacy
- listening skills
- managing our feelings and those of others
- being a safe listener
- understanding other people's worlds, i.e. developing empathy
- defining and asserting ourselves
- the concept of personal responsibility
- avoiding collusion
- managing our stress and anger
- setting realistic rules for ourselves
- handling criticism
- managing conflict in relationships
- peer support systems
- solution focused ideas
- teacher coaching
- exception finding
- preferred futures
- self-knowledge and reflection skills
- causes of challenging behaviour
- identifying what we can influence
- developing high quality and effective classroom practice
- increasing our coping strategies and support options

I would suggest that we make use of this list but also that we clarify any areas covered for each other that may seem still unclear at this point in time. It would be helpful if one person could act as a scribe and record all our views, thoughts and feelings.

Activity 2

Action Plan

In this activity it will be helpful to refer back to the questionnaire that you completed in Module 7 entitled 'Looking at your own Style and Attitude' and to also refer to the take home task entitled 'Emotional Literacy Exercise' that you completed at the end of Module 1. The idea here is to begin to reflect on what you feel you have gained from the course, whilst also identifying any changes that you may have made in terms of both your own level of emotional literacy and your personal skills and attitudes within the classroom context. Do you now feel differently? Do you feel more confident? Do you feel that you have developed strategies which will enable you to be more effective in terms of managing the behaviour of even the most difficult of students?

What is it that you now need to do in order to become more effective and more confident? You can complete the action plan where you are required to enter details of the specific action that you may utilise in order to further improve your behaviour management. You can then give reasons for this action, i.e. describe exactly why you have chosen to do this and what the outcome should be. It is also essential to identify pre-requisites for implementation. It may be that there are some preliminary steps which must be taken in order for you to achieve your goal. For example, referring to your Head of Department in order to change the specific policy within the department, the purchase of specific equipment, adapting a timetable, access to peer mentoring or support, access to team teaching opportunities etc. Finally, you can specify a start and first review date and also clarify with whom you will be reviewing your action plan.

The review format is provided and can clearly be used on further occasions, i.e. there does not have to be one review. In fact I would suggest that behaviour management skills needs to be continually developed and honed in line with changes and differences in the target groups that you will be teaching. It is, therefore, essential that any action plan is reviewed on an ongoing basis when new goals and activities are identified.

I hope that this will be a useful process and become part of the school systems for supporting teachers to become confident, emotionally literate and skilled in this key area of behaviour management. I hope that the training objectives have been met and that you feel now more able to manage every classroom context that you come into. I also hope that you have developed your own self-knowledge and awareness, your skills of emotional literacy and awareness of the ways in which you manage the learning within your classroom. I also hope that you are now able to identify with more confidence the root causes of challenging behaviour and to discriminate between what you can directly influence and what you can only influence indirectly. I also hope that you now feel confident in demonstrating high quality and effective classroom practice and that your teaching and classroom behaviour management show evident improvement as a result of this series of modules.

Most importantly, I hope that you now feel that you have the skills to assess and cope with even the most difficult situations and that the repertoire of skills you have developed can be fostered on an ongoing basis within the context of an emotionally literate and supportive staff team.

MODULE 8

Emotionally Literate Behaviour Management

ACTION PLAN

Refer back to the Emotional Literacy Questionnaire, your styles and Attitudes Questionnaire etc. and try to identify specific ACTIONS for yourself.

ACTION

Enter details of the action (e.g. alternate boys and girls in a specific class)

REASONS FOR ACTION: Describe why you've chosen to do this (e.g. a troublesome class very prone to gossiping and squabbling)

HOW DOES IT SUPPORT THE SCHOOL DEVELOPMENT PLAN?

PREREQUISITES FOR IMPLEMENTATION: Enter any preliminary steps which must be taken (e.g. refer to dept. head to change department policy, purchase equipment, adapt timetable)

Start date

First review due and by whom

FIRST REVIEW

Effects noted: Describe improvements/deterioration observed with date of observation and suggested reasons if any (e.g. small reduction in low-level disruption but 2 individuals now spend time flirting – dd/mm/yy)

Changes/additions to action if any: (e.g. separate 2 flirting individuals)

Next review due

Printed in the United Kingdom
by Lightning Source UK Ltd.
128312UK00001B/55/P